The Deltic Years

The Deltic Years

From prototype to preservation

HUGH W. WATSON

PSL

Patrick Stephens Limited

First published in 1989

British Library Cataloguing in Publication Data

Watson, Hugh W.
  The Deltic years.
  1. Great Britain. Railway services : British Rail. Deltic Class diesel-electric locomotives, to 1981
  I. Title
  625.2'662'0941

  ISBN 1-85260-095-0

Patrick Stephens Limited is part of the Thorsons Publishing Group, Wellingborough, Northamptonshire, NN8 2RQ, England

Printed in Great Britain by Butler & Tanner Limited, Frome, Somerset

10 9 8 7 6 5 4 3 2 1

Contents

The Deltic Years in Colour: special feature between pages 64 and 65

'Farewell *Pinza*, old friend. We grew up and old together. I'm afraid the sands of time ran out for you, but in my heart you'll never be forgotten.'

Acknowledgements

The preparation of this book would have been impossible without the help of so many people, including Cecil J. Allen and O. S. Nock, whose logs of 'Deltic' runs I have referred to from time to time.

Sincere thanks to Mr David Carter who, without hesitation, allowed the use of his marvellous collection of 'Deltic' photographs and took a great deal of time preparing them for inclusion in this book.

A big thank you to Messrs N. Skinner, R. Newling-Goode, P. Crumpton, B. R. Macaulay, J. Flounders, D. Hardy, D. Allinson, J. W. Armstrong and unknown photographer(s) whose work(s) I have drawn upon from my personal collection acquired over the years.

Thanks to my friend, Terry Bye, for a photograph and encouragement in a most humorous manner. Special thanks to Simon Cholmondeley for putting his superb photographic collection at my disposal, and to Bob Peach for giving his permission to include information he gathered whilst employed by British Rail.

Thanks to the staff of British Rail, in particular certain 'Deltic' drivers from all four depots concerned.

Last, but by no means least, a big thank you to my wife, Linda, whose enthusiasm culminated in my notes being transferred to manuscript form and who endured many hours by my side collecting information or just watching the 'Deltics' roll by.

Introduction

During the mid-1950s, British Railways issued a modernization plan, a major part of which was to eradicate steam locomotives by a more efficient and cleaner means of propulsion. Since the late-1940s, the railways of Britain had gained valuable experience using diesel-electric motive power in the shape of the prototype London Midland and Southern Regions' main-line locomotives Nos 10000, 10001, 10201, 10202 and 10203. These diesel-electric locomotives proved to be quite reliable but were very heavy, cumbersome machines (weighing around 130 tons) and they lacked any sparkling performance even though producing around 2,000 hp. This power-to-weight ratio problem became very clear when these early prototypes were used on trains such as the 'Royal Scot'. This service, during the period concerned, was quite easily handled by one of Mr Stanier's 'Duchess' Class steam locomotives, but when the diesels were rostered to this duty they had to work in pairs in order to keep time.

Obviously, this problem had to be solved and it was from English Electric's Preston factory that the answer emerged. English Electric had for many years gained vast experience, being involved in the manufacture of marine craft utilizing 'Napier' lightweight, high-speed, 'delta' piston formation diesel engines. It was from this conception that English Electric's engineers designed a locomotive body of a suitable weight in which to install two 1,650 bhp diesel engines, each driving a main generator providing electric current to six axle-hung, nose-suspended traction motors, positioned in two three-axle bogies (a 'Co–Co' wheel arrangement). All this, together with a train heating boiler, fuel and water tanks etc, produced a 3,300 bhp diesel-electric locomotive weighing only 106 tons.

So it was that during October 1955, locomotive DP1, named *Deltic*, emerged from English Electric's Preston factory to begin exhaustive trials. Initially, DP1 was utilized on the London Midland Region, mainly between London and Liverpool. After modifications by English Electric, it was tested with a British Railways' mobile test unit over the

Settle to Carlisle line, before recommencing its previous London to Liverpool trains, clocking up 720 miles per day.

During early 1959, DP1 was allocated to Hornsey Depot, Eastern Region, where, during high-speed braking tests between King's Cross and Grantham, she attained more than 105 mph hauling a 355-ton train — a foretaste of the future. It was during this sojourn on the Eastern that the management of that region saw the answer to all their problems; the replacement of their very competent fleet of 'Pacific' steam locomotives by a fleet of 22 'Deltic' diesel-electrics.

So it was, during 1961 and after many modifications, that the production 'Deltic' was born — the beginning of an era which would never be surpassed by any other diesel locomotive.

*   *   *

The aim of this book is to portray the 'Deltics' in a way which has not yet been done in book form, that is to follow the almost daily workload and performance of the locomotives from their birthplace to the scrapyard and into preservation, trying to bring out each locomotive as an individual personality without getting bogged down in heavy technical data, so that the younger enthusiast or the non-technically minded can easily follow the story — a story which covers the places the 'Deltics' worked and visited, and the affection which was bestowed upon them, not only by the enthusiast but also by working railwaymen. And if my own personal liking for these machines comes through in the book, I make no apology!

1961

'...the 'Deltics' would restore the highest pre-war standards of passenger train speed...'

D9015 Tulyar *accelerates away from York on a down King's Cross to Glasgow train, leaving behind it the characteristic 'Deltic' exhaust trail* (N. Skinner).

The part of my life as a dedicated railway enthusiast associated with the 'Deltics' began on 2 September 1961. I shall never forget the sighting of my first 'Deltic' at Bradbury, Co Durham. I remember that 'A4' 'Pacific' No 60009 *Union of South Africa* had not long hurtled south on the 'Elizabethan', followed by a couple of 'K1' Class steam locomotives going north and '9F' 2-10-0 No 92140 unusually heading south on the 'Anglo-Scottish Car Carrier'. Then my eyes sighted an apparition heading north, resplendent in dark green livery complemented by a large light green band around the lower superstructure and white cab window surrounds extending to the roof ends. As the locomotive passed, running light at around 30 mph, it was identified as D9005, then un-

named and without the yellow warning panels which later embellished the ends. The nearby signal which had slowed its progress changed to green and then it happened — my first chance to sample that unmistakable roar and exhaust effect that was to become part of the 'Deltic' scene over the years ahead.

The first production series 'Deltics' were very soon accepted by British Rail staff, the public and enthusiast alike, and remained so throughout their existence. The first production unit to reach London was D9001, later *St Paddy*. It travelled up light engine on 17 January 1961 for a private exhibition at Stratford Motive Power Depot, along with 'Sulzer' Type 4 No D18 and 'Crompton' Type 3 No D6539. D9001 returned north again after the exhibition on 18 January.

Two production units were expected to be available for service on the Eastern Region by the end of February 1961 and thereafter deliveries would be one per fortnight. As well as D9001, D9000, later to become *Royal Scots Grey,* was delivered and ready for service by late February 1961. This loco had the unique feature of a flashing light fitted at both ends at buffer beam height to act as a warning device to railmen and public alike. This device was tested in the area around Hadley Wood on 10 March 1961, but was removed during August.

D9001 was at King's Cross on 15 March at the head of a dynamometer-car test train to Doncaster and, from lineside observers' reports, demonstrated that the performance of the prototype had been fully reproduced in the production series version. Earlier that month, D9001 had been employed on the King's Cross to Doncaster diagram of the prototype 'Deltic', beginning with the 08.25 to Hull as far as Doncaster. D9001 apparently made light work of the job and on 8 March was noted passing Hatfield five minutes early.

During March it became known that Gateshead Depot was to become Tyneside's principal diesel depot and so it was allocated its first 'Deltic', No D9002, later to be named *The King's Own Yorkshire Light Infantry.* By the end of the month, the Gateshead 'Deltics' began crew-training, D9002 being noted at Carlisle on a parcels train which, until well into April 1961, was a favourite 'Deltic' crew-training turn.

By Easter 1961 D9002 had arrived at Neville Hill Depot, Leeds, after working in on a test train on 29 March. Later it returned north to Newcastle via Harrogate and Ripon and became the first 'Deltic' to use that route before the class took up regular duties on such trains as the 'Queen of Scots'.

The following month, Eastern Region began to run into trouble with both 'Deltics' and the smaller 'English Electric' Class '37' Co-Co's with complaints involving bogie frames, and all locomotives were stopped pending investigation. By this time, the latest 'Deltic' completed was D9004, later to become *Queen's Own Highlander.* After rigorous investigation, D9001 returned to Eastern Region traffic on 26 April after modifications which were subsequently carried out on all existing 'Deltics', Class 37s and those yet to be built.

During the same month the sad news was announced that the proto-

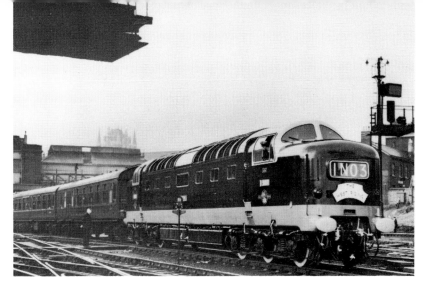

D9001 St Paddy *leaves King's Cross with the 'West Riding' service for Leeds Central, August 1961.*

type 'Deltic' would never run again as it had sustained a piston failure whilst working a King's Cross to Doncaster service during March, badly damaging one engine. Years later, after seeing it incarcerated in the Science Museum, London, I deplored that this magnificent locomotive would never again see the outside world in service, but thank goodness that it was preserved at all after the ignominious fate suffered by other prototypes.

During April, British Rail decided to hold an exhibition in Marylebone Goods Yard featuring both goods stock and locomotives. Of course the exhibition had to include a 'Deltic', so D9003 *Meld* was sent over from Finsbury Park Depot together with 'A4' 'Pacific' No 60022 *Mallard* to represent Eastern Region. Other types on show were: 'Hymek' Type 3 D7000; '9F' No 92220 *Evening Star*; '8P' No 71000 *Duke of Gloucester*; 'Midland Compound' No 1000; and the experimental gas turbine loco GT3.

After being exhibited at several locations, it was not too long before the 'Deltics' became firm favourites amongst the railway enthusiast fraternity, not only because of their good looks but also because of their sheer power and speed. The latter was to become their trademark, and by mid-1961 the class was beginning to settle down to become one of the most successful stories in British railway history.

In the August edition of *Trains Illustrated*, Cecil J. Allen told of the following run on a test train headed by D9001 *St Paddy* over the Great Northern main line between King's Cross and Doncaster. Schedule times had been calculated by the operating authorities for an 'all-out' performance with the full 3,300 rated hp hauling an eleven-coach load, and remarkably accurate these times proved to be. They took into account an official relaxation of certain normal speed restrictions in use at that time such as, for example, 70 to 80 mph round the Offord curves and up to 100 mph over various sections where 90 mph was the limit. The booked times for the run of 155.95 miles were 130 mins down and 126 mins up, but these included recovery times to compensate for permanent way slacks; the net allowance in both directions was 120 mins, demanding a start-to-stop average speed of a fraction under 78 mph

D9003 Meld *makes an unscheduled stop at Darlington Bank Top hauling the up 'Flying Scotsman' on a dull, overcast day in 1961.*

each way. The trailing load was 373 tons tare and 380 tons gross.

The start from King's Cross was quite rapid up the 1 in 105-110 to Holloway, topping this initial climb at 43 mph and passing the centre of Finsbury Park Station in 4 mins 33 secs at 57 mph. Up the long 1 in 200 to Potters Bar, 75 mph was maintained, D9001 taking 13 mins 19 secs to this point. From Potters Bar to Woolmer Green, D9001 had to be kept in check to conform to speed limits, thus the speed was 84 mph beyond Hatfield and 81 mph at Woolmer Green. At Brookmans Park there was a moderate relaying check to 42 mph, but so rapid was the recovery that D9001 reached 84 mph just beyond Hatfield and probably lost no more than 45 secs. Now, once again, having just topped the 100 mph mark before Hitchin, D9001 was kept under restraint and so ran between 99 and 102 mph from Hitchin to Sandy, averaging 99.2 mph over the 15.6 miles. So, Sandy was passed in 34 mins 57 secs which included, of course, the loss of time occasioned by the Brookmans Park relaying check.

Beyond Sandy, D9001 had a second slowing, this time a bad one to 14 mph and another to 77 mph round the Offord curves and 70-69 mph across Stilton Fen from Holme to Yaxley. D9001 touched 98 mph beyond St Neots and 94 mph at Conington South, falling only from 87 to 82 mph up the 1 in 200 from Huntingdon to milepost 62, and passed Peterborough in 61 mins 19 secs, or 57 mins 45 secs net. Beyond Peterborough again came the restraint imposed due to the then speed limits prevailing as far as Werrington Junction; D9001 then opened out again but to a rather more leisurely recovery than from the previous slacks. Up the stretches of 1 in 264 and level to Little Bytham, speed was kept at a steady 86 to 88 mph; the minimum up the 1 in 200 before Corby was 83 mph with a recovery to 85 mph through that station. Up the final 3 miles at 1 in 178 speed fell to 81 mph.

The Brookmans Park speed restriction had been eased since the schedule calculations for this test run had been made, with the result that D9001 had gained 2 mins to Hatfield. From there onwards very slight economies on the point-to-point allowances, a few seconds at a time, had put D9001 4 mins ahead by Werrington Junction. A top speed of 101 mph near Claypole increased the advantage to 4½ mins at Newark, while beyond the 67 mph speed restriction over Muskham troughs there came one of the lightning accelerations which were a feature of the day, to 91 mph beyond Carlton. Markham Summit was taken by storm as though it was not there, with nothing less than 83.5 mph up the 1 in 200 to Dukeries Junction and 98 mph before slowing for the Retford Crossing, which was still in position at that time. There was a further curb on speed between Retford and Doncaster — slacks imposed 60 mph at Scrooby troughs, 15 mph for the Bawtry Viaduct rebuilding and 26 mph for relaying at Rossington. Nevertheless, D9001 came to a stand in Doncaster Station in 125 mins 8 secs, or 117 mins net, from King's Cross, representing a start-to-stop speed of an average of almost 80 mph with this 380-ton train.

The scene was now firmly set for the great things to come from this small but substantial class. Although mostly confined to the East Coast Main Line in 1961, the 'Deltics' made sorties from time to time for various reasons, mainly due to engineering works. Thus, on 4 June, D9001 made a first appearance for the 'Deltics' at Lincoln when it passed through on the 08.20 King's Cross to Edinburgh, diverted because of engineering work at Newark.

During the summer, the 'Deltics' also began some long-distance work — for example, a Haymarket loco brought up the morning 'Talisman' and returned on the 'Aberdonian' Mondays to Fridays. On Saturdays the loco worked up with the 'Flying Scotsman', which on Tuesdays to Fridays at that time was a Gateshead Type 4 duty. In fact, the first regular duty entrusted to Haymarket 'Deltics' was the 11.00 Edinburgh to King's Cross as far as Newcastle, returning on the 11.00 King's Cross to Glasgow as far as Edinburgh.

Notable sightings of 'Deltics' off their beaten tracks during July were D9007 *Pinza* at Beattock on 5 July, seen running light apparently on clearance tests, and D9008, later to be named *The Green Howards*, noted on 29 July at Brampton Junction on the Saturdays-only Ayr to Newcastle train, which it hauled onwards from Carlisle during a driver-training programme.

Throughout the year the word had spread along the East Coast Main Line that the 'Deltics' would restore the highest pre-war standards of passenger train speed between London, the West Riding, Tyneside and Scotland. Originally, it was hoped that these production units would be in service by the beginning of the summer timetable, but due to late deliveries this was made impossible. Then the above mentioned bogie defects came to light on the earlier units, and although these were soon remedied, trial running, driver training and deliveries of the later units were inevitably retarded to such a degree that the operating

*D9013 (then un-named but later
The Black Watch) passes
York on the up 'Talisman',
7 August 1961* (D. Hardy).

authorities could only depend on fourteen locos being ready for the winter 1961 timetable. However, since the remedy of the bogie defects, no problems of any consequence were encountered and the 'Deltics' began fully to justify all expectations of performance and reliability. Although some crews complained about cab noise, it did not stop them from taking an enthusiastic approach to their new mounts.

So, the winter timetable got off to a disappointing start without the expected 22 'Deltics', but the East Coast Main Line was still able to accelerate drastically five of its principal trains. This was no more than ten per cent of the improvements originally planned and meant that fewer 'Deltics' were running their optimum weekly mileage. Their fuel capacity was adequate for return trips between King's Cross and Leeds or Newcastle without time off for refuelling, though not for a King's Cross to Edinburgh return trip, so in the first two cases the locomotives could, if required, be run round their trains in the stations. The safe turn-round allowance where refuelling was required was 45 minutes, but here again it was dependent upon other factors. Undoubtedly, this acceleration of services facilitated better utilization of coaching stock — for example, a single set of coaches could be used for a day's out and home working between King's Cross and Edinburgh.

After August, some changes to the 'Deltic' diagrams took place. On Tuesdays and Fridays, for example, the up 'Flying Scotsman' was worked by the London 'Deltic' off the previous night's 22.15 to Aberdeen. At the same time, Gateshead 'Deltics' began Mondays to Fridays duty on the 07.56 Newcastle to King's Cross and down afternoon 'Talisman', or the 08.52 and 17.53 down on Saturdays. Gateshead 'Deltics' were also observed on the 'Tees-Tyne Pullman' and night car sleeper.

Autumn 1961 brought with it reports of varying power output between different members of the class. For example, D9009 *Alycidon* was found to be unable to exceed 80 mph on the climb to Stoke, which other 'Deltics' had breasted repeatedly at a greater speed with the same load. On 26 October, D9009 was 'short of amps' on the up afternoon 'Sheffield Pullman' which was 'Deltic'-hauled for a short time, and was detached at Grantham in favour of a Class 'A3' 'Pacific' No 60102, which departed almost one hour late. The same day, D9015 *Tulyar* failed at Hatfield on the down evening 'Pullman' when a Class '31' had to be substituted. The previous day, the 25th, saw D9000, later *Royal Scots Grey*, unusually heading the up 'West Riding' before dealing with the down 'Talisman'.

Nonetheless, the month saw numerous through diesel workings between London and Edinburgh, mostly by Haymarket locomotives on the up morning 'Talisman' and down 'Aberdonian'; up 'Scotsman' and 22.15 from King's Cross; up 'Heart of Midlothian' and 23.35 from King's Cross and the 23.05 from Edinburgh and the down 'Flying Scotsman'. On one occasion during October, the 'Deltic' on the up 'Flying Scotsman' reached King's Cross 5 minutes early after being reported supposedly 55 minutes late passing Berwick. Also during October, a London 'Deltic' was responsible for the 11.00 from King's Cross and the 22.30 back from Edinburgh. A Gateshead 'Deltic' also travelled to King's Cross on the 07.50 from Newcastle, returning with the down 'Talisman', and another arrived on the 17.00 from Newcastle, returning on the 09.00, the down 'Tynesider'. It appeared during this time that the former double King's Cross to Doncaster 'Deltic' duty was now being used on occasion to provide a 'Deltic' as a reserve to guard against emergencies on other 'Deltic' turns in the Doncaster area. This involved the locomotive off the 08.15 King's Cross to Hull standing pilot at Doncaster until its return to King's Cross with an overnight Edinburgh parcels train. However, the 'Deltic' was diagrammed to return from Doncaster on the 11.50 ex Harrogate.

Towards the end of October, the 'Deltics' encountered a patch of misfortune when several of their normal turns had to be covered by steam locomotives. The most familiar source of trouble appeared to be the train heating boiler, with the result that steam once again returned to such trains as the 'Flying Scotsman' and 'Talisman'. It was reported that King's Cross 'A4' 'Pacifics' worked throughout to Edinburgh and back in a day. Meanwhile, at Doncaster Works, part of the Crimpsall Shops was adapted to deal with the periodic overhauls of all the 'Deltics'.

D9004 (then un-named but later
Queen's Own Highlander)
gets to grips with Holloway
Bank, heading the down 'Queen
of Scots' Pullman during
September 1961 (D. Carter
Collection).

During the late autumn, D9007 *Pinza*, with a 380-ton train (405
tons gross) and notwithstanding many delays, reached every stop ahead
of time whilst heading the 11.00 King's Cross to Glasgow. During the
run *Pinza* accelerated from 25 mph just before Hitchin to 96 mph by
Three Counties, a distance of around 4.5 miles; an acceleration from
York Station to 85 mph by Tollerton; and an unusual time of 21 mins
8 secs, including an easing to 58 mph round Aycliffe curve, for the 21.05
miles from the Darlington start to passing Relly Mill Junction, Durham
— all magnificent feats way back in 1961.

It is true to say that even at that time steam could do nothing to ap-

proach the climbing speeds of the 'Deltics' — *Sir Nigel Gresley*'s 82 mph minimum at Stoke Summit in May 1959 probably represented the limit with steam haulage and this was only with eight coaches of 271 tons. By comparison, D9001 *St Paddy* went up the 4.5 miles of 1 in 200 at a minimum of 90 mph and the final 3 miles of 1 in 178 with a speed drop of no greater than 2 mph. D9007 *Pinza* beat this with a 92 mph minimum on the former grade, touched no less than 95 mph on the short level past Corby Glen, and went over Stoke Summit at 90 mph, while D9012 *Crepello* also passed the summit at 86 mph. The truly staggering feat of *Pinza* was that of covering the entire 15.25 miles of the climb at an average speed of 92.7 mph. Another run with *Crepello*, hauling 410 tons, found it 6 minutes late passing Essendine due to permanent way slacks, but with speeds of 96 to 102 mph between Barkston and Newark, an acceleration from 70 mph at Muskham troughs to 93 mph on the level at Crow Park, 90 mph minimum up the 1 in 200 to Dukeries Junction and a final 96 mph before Retford, the net time on this run was 79.75 mins for the 106.7 miles from Hitchin to Retford. This meant a start-to-stop average of 80.3 mph and a gain of 9.25 mins on the schedule.

Towards the end of 1961, the first multiple collision involving a 'Deltic' occurred. On the night of 15 December, D9012 *Crepello* was at Conington heading the 21.51 Scotswood to Holloway goods when it apparently ran into the rear of the 21.50 New England to King's Cross goods. *Crepello* was derailed and seriously damaged; the wreckage fouled the up main line and was run into by 'V2' 2-6-2 No 60977, which also derailed, and in turn fouled the down main line. The final element of the disaster was the involvement of the 18.10 King's Cross to Newcastle goods, headed by 'A3' 'Pacific' No 60078, which was thrown on its side, thus blocking all the tracks. While breakdown gangs cleared the wreckage, all other main-line freight and passenger duties were diverted to other routes; as a result D9001 *St Paddy* had its first run along the March-St Ives-Cambridge loop and became the first 'Deltic' to pass that way.

During the 4-8 December period, the 'Sheffield Pullman' reverted to 'Deltic' haulage as loads had been increased to deal with extra passengers travelling to and from London on Christmas shopping trips.

The year came to an end in a blaze of glory for the 'Deltics'. However, the advent of diesels led to lines of redundant steam locomotives scattered about the East Coast running sheds awaiting their call to the scrapyard, a decision which upset avid steam enthusiasts.

Typical of the period, Gresley 'A3' 'Pacific' 60045 Lemberg is cut up at Draper's scrapyard, Hull.

1962

'...a frequency of express service without parallel in Europe over so great a distance...'

During January 1962, terrible winter conditions culminated in a big freeze which became a major problem on the East Coast Main Line. Many classes of diesels became unavailable including the 'Deltics', whose major problem appeared still to be the train heating boilers. On one day alone, no fewer than three units were failed on this score. In general it seemed to be the Finsbury Park and Haymarket units that were absent from work, and to overcome this problem, new experimental exhaust stacks were tried. During this difficult period, the Edinburgh duties were being worked by Haymarket's latest batch of Class '40's. In the bitter conditions at the beginning of the month, steam had to deputize on a number of occasions because of the late running of all traffic which resulted in the diesels not reaching their destinations in enough time to take up their next duty.

During the late January-early February period, 'Deltics' began through-working to Glasgow. One duty involved was the 17.15 Edinburgh to Glasgow and the 22.00 back, which included the Fort William to King's Cross sleepers. Other new ground was broken by the 'Deltics' on 11 March when, because of Sunday engineering works on the normal route between Wakefield and Doncaster, the 10.35 and 13.00 from Leeds, headed by D9016 (later named *Gordon Highlander*) and D9020 *Nimbus* respectively, were seen taking the Wakefield to Goole line to Knottingley and there diverging to join the East Coast Main Line at Shaftsholme Junction. There were similar diversions the following Sunday.

Towards the summer of 1962, the 'Deltics' had overcome most of their teething troubles and began to settle down to the hard work for which they were designed. With all 22 locomotives now delivered, the revised 'Deltic' timetable came into force on 18 June. Almost immediately it was noticed that the operating authorities of the three regions concerned had decided for the time being not to put into operation the complete set of rosters for the 'Deltics'. Instead, it was arranged to leave a rather wider margin between potential and actual utilization.

D9016 (then un-named but later Gordon Highlander) passes Thirsk on an unidentified special (D. Carter).

Until the teething period had completely ended, this ensured a reasonably certain 'Deltic' haulage of all the trains so scheduled — an essential provision, because with full loads timekeeping on the 'Deltic' turns would be difficult and, on the hardest, probably impossible with Type 4 diesel or 'Pacific' steam power. In the event, by careful arrangement the reduction in 'Deltic' workings had less effect on the timetable than was first expected.

Thus, the 'Deltics' began the summer timetable of 1962 with great vigour, tackling the vastly accelerated train services. The three six-hour flyers in each direction daily between King's Cross and Edinburgh produced some unprecedented results; the slogan 'King's Cross for Scotland' was totally justified by the fact that the East Coast Main Line now provided a faster service to all points in the east, centre and north of Scotland than the West Coast route. In fact, every day there were fifteen trains from King's Cross to Newcastle travelling the 268.4 miles in an average time of 4 hrs 59 mins — a frequency of express service without parallel in Europe over so great a distance at that time.

One instance of these accelerated timings was the 'Flying Scotsman' and, on its inaugural run to the north on 18 June, it was headed by D9020 *Nimbus* in pristine external condition. The eleven-coach load tared 393 tons plus passengers and luggage in a well-filled train, which brought the gross load up to 420 tons or 95 tons more than the pre-war 'Coronation'. Included in the 'Scotsman' were a number of vehicles with the latest type of bogie and a tare weight of 36 or 37 tons apiece, so that the total tare was actually 8 tons in excess of the specified 'Deltic' maximum of 385 tons for these timings.

South of York the schedule was eminently practical and it was clearly the aim of Driver Ellington to see that *Nimbus* stuck as closely to it as possible — indeed, the handling throughout to Newcastle was a model of precision. For this reason, *Nimbus* did not exceed 70 mph up the long 1 in 200 to Potters Bar. The restriction to 75 mph through Hatfield was continued until *Nimbus* was clear of Woolmer Green, and then at Biggleswade came another restriction which brought speed down to 20 mph, which consequently brought *Nimbus* down to 5 mins late on passing Sandy. Up the 1 in 200 beyond Sandy, *Nimbus* now accelerated to milepost 62 from 77 to 80.5 mph and then had to be brought down from 88 to 66 mph to conform to a speed restriction at Abbots Ripton. *Nimbus* passed through Peterborough 1 min early despite these setbacks.

After Peterborough began a most convincing demonstration of the superior power output of a 'Deltic' on the long climb up to Stoke Summit. From Essendine up to milepost 95.5 (the last 4 miles at 1 in 200), *Nimbus*, with 420 tons, was maintaining 90-85 mph, and on the final three miles at 1 in 178 the 'Deltic' maintained 88 down to a minimum of 85 mph. By Grantham, therefore, the arrears in time had been reduced by 5 mins and the 'Flying Scotsman' was then 1.75 mins early.

North of Grantham, *Nimbus* suffered another bad permanent way check at Barkston, at Bawtry Viaduct and a really long 40 mph slowing between Doncaster and Arksey, but between these checks D9020 continued to show its superiority in both acceleration and hill climbing, proof being the 83.5–82.5 mph up to Markham Summit and from 32 to 59 mph in two miles up to Pipers Wood. However, *Nimbus* lost nearly 3 mins between Black Carr Junction and Shaftsholme Junction due to the long permanent way caution, but made up for this with some fine high-speed work along the subsequent level towards York, eventually passing York after an extremely cautious approach in 165 mins from King's Cross, just over 2 mins early.

Northwards from York, *Nimbus* had another bad permanent way slack near Thirsk and signal checks approaching Darlington, but even these could not deter D9020 from maintaining scheduled time, stopping in Newcastle Central Station in 239 mins 19 secs from King's Cross, 1.75 mins early. Allowing 4 mins for the bad Thirsk slowing, 1.5 mins for the Darlington signal check and 0.75 mins for a final check, the net time from King's Cross to Newcastle worked out at 222 mins, or 3 mins less than the scheduled 241 mins with the total 16 mins of recovery time deducted.

From Newcastle Central, *Nimbus* had a bad start for, as a result of slight mishandling, she crawled out of the platform and took no less than 6 mins 40 secs to clear Benton Bank box, 2.7 miles, thus dropping just over 1 min to Morpeth. Between Morpeth and Alnmouth, speed was allowed to rise to 95 mph on the level to Chevington, but then the 65 mph curve restriction near Warkworth was over-emphasized, and D9020 came down to 53 mph. 'Deltic' power was again seen in the acceleration from 60 to 75 mph up the 1 in 170 of Longhaughton Bank. After Alnmouth, hopes of high speed from Christon Bank to Beal were dashed by a 20 mph permanent way restriction at Smeafield, but the 3 min recovery here saw *Nimbus* through Tweedmouth just ahead of time. Unfortunately, there had been a minor derailment at Marshall Meadows on the previous day, which had affected the signalling, and signal checks at Tweedmouth and Berwick were succeeded by a dead

Un-named D9005 enters Newcastle Central on the up 'Talisman' on a dull, cold morning (H. Watson).

stand at Marshall Meadows box for 0.75 mins.

Up the climb from Berwick to Burnmouth, *Nimbus* accelerated from a dead start to 71.5 mph, but even so Reston was passed 3.75 mins late and worse was to come. A sudden restriction of speed for yet another permanent way check between Reston and Granthouse unexpectedly brought the train to a second dead stand, with the result that by Granthouse *Nimbus* was 6 mins late and, with no prospect of a punctual arrival, stopped in Waverley a shade under 5 mins late. Allowing 1 min for the permanent way check after Benton Bank, 2.5 mins for Smeafield, 5 mins for the Berwick troubles and 3 mins for the stop after Reston, the net time comes down to 109 mins or slightly less, and a normal start out of Newcastle would have cut this to 107.5 mins at most. As to the schedule, one excessive allowance is the 5.5 mins from Reston Junction to Granthouse — 1 min at least might well have been cut from this and conceded between Monktonhall and Edinburgh.

Adding the net running times together, *Nimbus* had therefore achieved a most praiseworthy figure of almost exactly 5.5 hrs, which works out at 71.4 mph throughout. It also shows that with the full eleven-coach load, these six-hour schedules with 'Deltic' haulage gave a reasonable margin for recovering all out-of-course delays other than those of abnormal character.

As already stated, the complete 22 locomotives were ready for the summer timetable of 1962. The last of the production 'Deltics', D9021, was noted at Longsight Depot, Manchester, at the end of March, and was later seen making nocturnal runs on the Manchester to Crewe line between two 25 kV AC electric locomotives at speeds of up to 100 mph. These tests were not connected with the running of the locomotives, but with comprehensive track tests that were in progress for some time at Heald Green under the aegis of the British Transport Commission

Research Department. D9021 was completely dead with motor brush gear removed and was positioned between the two electric locomotives prior to the test runs for the purpose of rail and stress tests. The locomotive eventually reached Doncaster Works in March to undergo acceptance tests.

The summer of 1962 also brought further joyous tidings for the 'Deltics'. Nameplates for D9000 were ready at St Rollox, Glasgow, by 8 May and the locomotive was expected into the works there on that day, although it was still not seen carrying nameplates by the end of May. D9000 was finally named *Royal Scots Grey* at a ceremony at Edinburgh's Waverley Station on 18 June, before heading the inaugural re-scheduled southbound 'Flying Scotsman' to King's Cross. Another nice touch was that 18 June happened to be the centenary of the 'Flying Scotsman' train service. These highlights of June 1962 were wonderful times for the 'Deltics', but not so for the now-declining steam locomotives.

Earlier, on 2 June, a special train had left King's Cross for Aber-

In pristine condition during those wonderful early years, D9015 Tulyar *stands at Retford* (D. Carter).

deen to mark the end of regular steam on the principal expresses. It departed from King's Cross headed by 'A4' 'Pacific' 60022 *Mallard* simultaneously with 'Deltic' D9016 from an adjacent platform — and what a sight they made disappearing into Gasworks Tunnel with the 'Deltic' gradually pulling away from the 'A4'.

By the end of June, the 'Deltics' had really settled into the six-hour King's Cross to Edinburgh services. In their first week, 24 of the 30 six-hour trips had arrived on time, and the maximum lateness recorded, as a result of mishap to another train ahead, had been no more than 12 mins. One reporter summed it up well when he wrote 'On one run, as the afternoon "Talisman" sped through the Vale of York in the nineties and met its opposite number doing roughly the same speed in the opposite direction, one felt a real pride in the "Deltics" as Edinburgh had been left on time and five minutes gained to Newcastle. A slight upset at Newcastle resulted in a seven minutes late departure but, despite a succession of permanent way checks between Doncaster and Newark, arrival at King's Cross was still five minutes early, 268.3 miles in 228 mins gross.'

Another point of interest was that during that summer new double-

D9016 (later named Gordon Highlander) *climbs past Holloway on a morning King's Cross to Leeds service in March 1962* (D. Carter Collection).

decked car carriers were introduced and used intensively. By employing 'Deltic' haulage on the night services, it was possible to cover both the overnight Holloway to Perth car sleeper and the daytime 'Anglo-Scottish Car Carrier' in each direction with only two sets of vehicles. On arrival at Edinburgh, the vehicles off the daytime service were worked to Perth for the overnight up working and vice versa in the opposite direction. It was these services which brought the first sightings of 'Deltics' in Perth.

A sad reflection on the 1962 summer timetable concerned the British non-stop record of the 'Elizabethan' service between King's Cross and Edinburgh, which was forced into making a stop at Newcastle Central for a crew change, thus losing the distinction of making a non-stop run of 392.75 miles. It was gathered at the time that the London crews involved were prepared to pass the whole journey time in the rather noisy cab of the 'Deltic', whether on or off duty, but it appeared that their northern colleagues were not so amenable to the idea.

Despite the fact that a week before the accelerated summer timetable all the 'Deltics' had undergone a searching examination, there were still a small number of failures. On 19 June, the up 'Heart of Midlothian' lost 18 mins between Newcastle and Grantham with Class '40' No D362 in charge of a 'Deltic' turn. On the following Saturday, the 08.00 Newcastle to King's Cross had 'A4' 'Pacific' No 60029 *Woodcock* running 25 mins late, and the 09.55 had 'English Electric' Class '40' D393 in charge. On the Monday, the up 'Flying Scotsman' arrived at King's Cross behind a Class '40' and the next day 'A3' 'Pacific' No 60112 *St Simon* had to take over the down 'Tees-Tyne Pullman' from D9017 at Greatford. The same day, the up 'Heart of Midlothian' reached King's Cross behind 'A3' 'Pacific' No 60105, followed some time later by D9006 running light engine.

On the whole, these failures were all only minor problems soon solved to leave the way ahead open to one of the most reliable traction units to use the rails in this country. By July, the 'Deltics' were very much in command with still fewer failures. At Welwyn, on 14 July, all the 'Deltics' were on time or running early — one unit on the 'Queen of Scots' was 20 mins early and no fewer than 16 units were spotted between 09.30 and 20.00. In fact, throughout the 1962 summer timetable, 'Deltic' performance did not diminish, but went from strength to strength.

On 7 September there was a freight train collision at Offord, so on the following day D9011 took 5 hrs 50 mins to reach Newcastle from King's Cross with the 'Flying Scotsman' as a result of travelling between Hitchin and Doncaster via Cambridge, Ely, March and Lincoln. The train stood at Newcastle Central for 14 mins, but after departure D9011 made considerable haste, covering the 121 miles to passing Portobello in 97 mins. No doubt at that time other 'Deltics' passed this way, as this route over the years has always been a popular diversionary route for the 'Deltics' among all the other East Coast diesel classes.

The advent of the 1962 winter timetable saw that the fine pro-

D9018 Ballymoss departs from York on the down 'Heart of Midlothian', 24 April 1962 (N. Skinner).

gramme of accelerations introduced in the summer were being continued unchanged except for the customary withdrawal of the 'Elizabethan'. Besides the 'Elizabethan', one of the fastest crack expresses of the summer, one of the more exacting duties was the Saturday 'Flying Scotsman', with its load increased on summer Saturdays from 11 to 13 coaches, although its timing between King's Cross and Edinburgh was eased to 6.5 hours. On this service, the 'Deltics', as with every other task put before them, performed admirably as can be gathered by the following run.

On the particular Saturday in question, the 'Scotsman' had a load of 485 tons gross headed by D9011. Following delays south of Newcastle, D9011 left Tyneside for Edinburgh 24 mins behind time with 123 mins (7 mins more than on other days) allowed for the 124.45 miles to the Scottish capital. However, with Driver R. Currie of Haymarket Depot at the controls, such an astonishing performance was put up that, despite a signal delay costing 1.75 mins, the train stopped in Waverley no more than 3.75 mins late. Items of note on this run were the 74 mph minimum up the 4 miles of 1 in 170 to Little Mill, the acceleration from 50 to 68 mph up the long 1 in 190 from Berwick, and the sustained 79–76 mph up the 1 in 200 to Granthouse — yet, of course, such figures and even higher speeds were common with 'Deltics' at that time up the 1 in 200 banks of the Great Northern main line.

The major speed restrictions were carefully observed, though over one or two sections the travelling was rather more lively than expected; the top speed was just over 95 mph at Smeafield, immediately before the one signal check. The way the operating authorities managed to keep the road clear for such time recovery on a busy Saturday was beyond praise and the energetic driving resulted in an actual gain of just over 20 mins and a net gain of 22 mins on schedule — 124.45 miles in 101 mins.

By the end of October, a second Class '47', or 'Brush 4' Co-Co, took to the East Coast Main Line and joined its sister, D1500, at

Finsbury Park Depot. On 10-11 October, what appeared to be comparative trials with a 'Deltic' were conducted with D1500 between King's Cross and Doncaster with a train of 385 tons. A schedule of 2 hrs 20 mins was specified for the down journey and one of 2 hrs 14 mins for the up, which terminated at Finsbury Park. On the first day, D9018 *Ballymoss* was used, and D1500 on the second day. The outcome of these trials was never published as far as I know, but Class '47's have always been the choice in the advent of a 'Deltic' failure, at times putting up truly magnificent performances.

As 1962 came to a close it was reported that Leeds Central Station was to be closed on Sundays, all traffic using City Station, where D9012 *Crepello* arrived on the up 'Yorkshire Pullman' on 21 October. This marked the beginning of the final run-down of Leeds Central.

1963

'Throughout the summer, 'Deltic' performance remained at a very high standard...'

The beginning of 1963 saw for the first time in British railway history a timetable containing a run scheduled at a start-to-stop speed of over 75 mph — it was that of the 'Tees-Tyne Pullman' between Darlington and York, a distance of 44.1 miles in 35 mins. Indeed, this stretch of line had no rival for freedom from curvature and gradients other than the main line from Swindon to Reading, 41.3 miles. It must also be added that at this time Eastern Region, in addition to its 35-min booking, had another at 36 mins and no fewer than six trains at 37 mins, all at more than 70 mph start-to-stop. The 75.6 mph timing was not merely practical but even had a small margin for recovery, always provided that the train was, of course, 'Deltic'-hauled.

On the 35-min run of the 'Tees-Tyne Pullman', comprising 8 coaches, D9005 accelerated up the 1 in 391 from Croft to Eryholme from 77 to 89 mph; after the slack at Wiske Moor troughs, high speeds ruled and finally reached 100 to 101 mph from Alne to Beningborough. Except for the extremely cautious approach to York (the train had to cross to the platform lines in the centre of the station), this run might have been accomplished in 32.5 mins start-to-stop, and this with 325 tons of train.

On another occasion, with 360 tons, D9017 reached 78.5 mph from the Darlington start in no more than 2.5 miles, then touched 100 mph at Danby Wiske before the trough slack; from Thirsk to Beningborough speed averaged 98.1 mph for 16.65 miles of practically level track, York being reached in 33.5 mins from Darlington at an average speed of 80 mph exactly.

At about this time further south, 'Deltics' were also showing their paces on the more testing parts of the East Coast Main Line. For instance, on the 'Aberdonian' loaded to 530 tons, D9016 maintained 69.5 to 70 mph all the way up the 1 in 200 from Wood Green to Potters Bar, thereby gaining nearly 3.5 mins on the schedule out of King's Cross. Still more remarkable was the 85–90 mph of D9006 from Tallington to Little Bytham, with nothing lower than 71 mph up the final 1 in 178 to Stoke Summit, and this also with 530 tons of train, thus showing the

D9017 The Durham Light Infantry *eases into King's Cross on the up 'Talisman' from Edinburgh* (D. Carter).

During the 1963 cold spell, D9019 (later Royal Highland Fusilier*) passes York on the up 'Flying Scotsman'* (D. Carter).

behaviour of 'Deltics' with really heavy trains.

During early 1963 it was severely cold, and it seemed that the North Eastern authorities were disinclined to entrust passengers to the mercy of the train heating equipment of the 'Deltics', which at about this period was giving further trouble. Gateshead units were noted on main-line fitted freights, and one was seen heading the Cliffe to Uddingston cement train from York to Heaton Yard, Newcastle. As usual, the 'Deltics' received priority treatment and the train heating boiler trouble was soon eradicated.

D9008 The Green Howards
*after being named at Darlington
Bank Top, 30 September 1963.*

During January, Haymarket 'Deltic' D9013 was admitted to St
Rollox Works, Glasgow, for new cast aluminium nameplates and
regimental crests to be fitted. The name chosen was the now legendary
The Black Watch, and on 16 January D9013 ran light to Dundee West
Station for a ceremonial naming. After the ceremony, it left light-engine
for Edinburgh via the coast route to take on the 16.00 for King's Cross
the same day. Later, in the spring of 1963, D9002 of Gateshead was
named *The King's Own Yorkshire Light Infantry*, while on 28 May D9011
was named *The Royal Northumberland Fusiliers* at a ceremony at Newcastle
Central. The remainder of the Gateshead allocation were all named
later in 1963; D9008 was named *The Green Howards* at a ceremony at
Darlington on 30 September and D9005 became *The Prince of Wales's
Own Regiment of Yorkshire* at York on 8 October. The last two Gateshead
'Deltics' to named were D9014, *The Duke of Wellington's Regiment*, and
D9017, which became *The Durham Light Infantry* at a ceremony at
Durham Station during October. In Scotland on 29 November, D9021
became *Argyll and Sutherland Highlander* at a ceremony held at Stirling.

By 1963 the 'Deltics' were beginning to be fairly regular performers on the King's Cross trains via the coast route through
Sunderland and Hartlepool. The most regular 'Deltic' turn via this
route was the Sundays-only 13.10 Newcastle to King's Cross, which
departed Hartlepool at around 14.15. On this train during 1963, 14
'Deltics' were noted (D9001/2/3/5/7/8/9/11/12/14/15/17/18 and 20).
Examination of these numbers points to the notable absence of
Haymarket-based locomotives, which might suggest that these 'Deltics'
were not diagrammed for this service.

With the 'Deltics' now receiving proper maintenance and all
teething troubles left in the past, evidence now pointed to the fact that
with diesel power the East Coast Main Line had locomotives to handle

timetables that, as far as harder assignments were concerned, would have been impossible to maintain with any steam power built up to that date. It must also be stated that in 1963 the 'Deltics' were now speed-restricted over various sections of the East Coast Main Line than was the case in earlier years. For example, the main line out of King's Cross had such limitations as 60 mph from start to beyond New Southgate; 70 mph from Hatfield to Woolmer Green; 65 mph from Holme to Yaxley; 60 mph from Peterborough to Werrington Junction; 70 mph through Grantham and for most of the way from Retford to Doncaster (with 55 mph through the latter station); and several others which were unknown in the streamliner days of 1935 to 1939.

Even so, in 1963 the 'Deltics' had charge of the fastest scheduled run in this country for a distance of over 100 miles, that of the 'West Riding' service between Hitchin and Retford. 'Deltic' performance on this turn was impeccable as is demonstrated in the following log of D9012 *Crepello*. On this run, D9012 had a train of eleven coaches of 400 gross tons on a schedule of 89 mins, which had been reduced to 88 mins,

D9003 Meld *accelerates away from York on the down 'Flying Scotsman'* (D. Carter Collection).

bringing the scheduled start-to-stop from a best of 66.7 mph in steam days up to 72.8 mph. Between Conington and Yaxley there were two permanent way checks, and even if the then-65 mph imposed on the speed of D9012 had been observed between Holme and Yaxley, the net time would not have been more than 83.5 minutes. Note also D9012's start, 5.2 miles in 5 mins 15 secs, with 87 mph already attained and an average of 94.2 mph maintained over the 14.65 miles from Arlesey to St Neots. Equally exciting was D9012's 81 mph minimum at Stoke Summit and later 89 mph passing Crow Park; thus *Crepello* passed Retford, 106.70 miles from Hitchin, in 86.32 mins, a minimum net time of 82 mins.

The 'Elizabethan' no longer appeared in the 1963 summer timetable. It will be recalled that 1961 was the last summer of non-stop running between London and Edinburgh with steam, and in 1962 a stop at Newcastle Central had to be made for a crew-change because of diesel haulage. In 1963, as the 'Flying Scotsman' had so great a reputation with the travelling public, it was difficult to lure sufficient passengers from it to fill the 'Elizabethan', so it was planned to use the latter as an un-named relief to the 'Scotsman'. By this time the 'Deltics' were making the return London and Edinburgh journey in one day — 786 miles all told.

Another feature of the summer timetable was an even-interval service, probably unequalled in any part of the world over such great distances. From King's Cross there was an express to Newcastle at exactly hourly intervals from 08.00 to 18.00, and to Edinburgh there were departures at 08.00, 10.00, 10.10, 11.00, 12.00, 14.00 and 16.00. From Edinburgh, starting times were 08.00, 09.00, 10.00, 11.00, 12.00, 13.30 and 16.00, while from Newcastle departures were roughly at hourly intervals — 7.50, 9.00, 10.04, 11.01, 11.58, 12.40, 13.12, 14.09, 15.39, 17.00 and 17.58. On the Leeds run, the times were not as speedy because of fairly numerous intermediate stops, though here again with 'Deltic' haulage a number of trains were substantially accelerated.

This timetable proved very successful. On 13 July, for example, it was noted that at Sandy between 10.00 and 17.00, only six of the long-distance expresses passed behind time; of these, four were the first seen, and of the remaining trains almost all were running up to 10 mins early. Also during this period there were some spectacular double-heading of Saturday workings between Leeds and Doncaster to facilitate locomotive movements; both the 16.49 stopping train and the 17.30 from Leeds were scheduled for a 'Deltic' and Class '47' combination — such high power was also noted elsewhere on the East Coast Main Line around this time.

By August 1963, the normal flow of steam-hauled expresses had all but disappeared and such classes as the 'A4' 'Pacifics' had now become a rarity in the Darlington area. Instead, 'Deltics', among other classes of diesels, were in abundance. On Saturday 28 August, D9002/7/8/9/ 10/12/13/14 and 15 were observed and also DP2 for good measure. Of course, sightings were not always as good as this — during a visit for a few hours to Newcastle Central early in July, only 'Deltics' D9005, D9013 and D9019 (then still un-named) had been noted, which was fairly disappointing.

At this point it is worth describing a run which Cecil J. Allen made behind D9005 out of King's Cross during 1963: by the time that the first 5 miles out of the terminus had been completed, all his previous records had been broken. D9005, having reached 60 mph as early as Finsbury Park with a 340-ton train, was up to no less than 80 mph by Wood Green with a continuing 80-82 mph all the way up the 1 in 200. D9005 was through Hatfield in 16 mins 28 secs from the dead start — Mr Allen's fastest time ever up to that date. There was not much doubt that D9005 could have equalled *Silver Link*'s 1935 sprint from Hatfield onwards had the diesel been allowed to do so, but it was not until after several speed checks that there was the rapid acceleration after Stevenage that finally gave D9005 an average of 99.7 mph over the 19.85 miles from Hitchin to St Neots, with several miles between Biggleswade and Tempsford covered at 102-103 mph. Then followed further checks and restraints from 60 down to 55 mph across Stilton Fen, not to mention a speed as low as 18 mph through Peterborough North Station. After yet another check there was, once again, a 'Deltic' demonstration that no 'A4' 'Pacific' would have been able to rival with a 340-ton train, speed being maintained unbrokenly at between 92 and 85 mph from Little Bytham up to Stoke Summit. D9005 was now 10 minutes ahead of time — a truly magnificent peformance only marred by the driver's disregard for passing Stoke Summit early, or should I say allowing D9005 to get 10 minutes ahead of schedule?

Throughout the summer, 'Deltic' performance remained at a very high standard and, as the winter timetable came into force, it was good to record that the accelerated schedules over the East Coast Main Line, with the help of the 'Deltics', Class '47's and '46's, had proved perfectly

D9012 Crepello *heads north out of York on a down King's Cross to Glasgow service* (N. Skinner).

practical and so were continued into the winter almost without alteration. Seasonal summer trains, such as the 10.10 King's Cross to Edinburgh, the 09.00 Edinburgh to King's Cross, the 'Anglo-Scottish Car Carrier' and the 'Highland Car Sleeper' were withdrawn as usual.

During early September, the 'Sulzer' 2,750 hp prototype *Lion* was transferred to Eastern Region and was introduced on a turn covering the 16.00 King's Cross to Leeds and the next day's 'Yorkshire Pullman' return, thus entering into 'Deltic' territory for a short stay at least.

Another excellent 1963 'Deltic' performance, recorded again by Cecil J. Allen, was the 'Heart of Midlothian', on which D9004 was exhibiting what could be described as little more than typical running with the 'Deltics' at that time. D9004 had 460 gross tons on its tail and, after climbing Stoke Bank from a dead stand at Grantham, was carefully restricted down to the official ceiling then in force down Stoke Bank of 90 mph towards Peterborough. After Peterborough there came the climb up Abbots Ripton Bank, where D9004, having reached 90 mph, maintained a steady 83.5 mph on the upper part of this 4.5 miles of 1 in 200. Up the second bank at Arlesey, D9004 did well to maintain 76.5 mph after a severe signal check at Biggleswade, but by Three Counties was accelerating to 80 mph up the grade and reached a minimum of 77.5 mph on passing the summit of this 1 in 200 climb to Stevenage. Mr Allen estimated that D9004 had brought the 460-ton train up over the 105.45 miles from Grantham to King's Cross in 92 mins 14 secs actual time start-to-stop, and had attained a net time of about 87.5 mins, or the equivalent of 85 mins net from passing Grantham at speed up to London. Performances such as this were now commonplace, and could be repeated any day by any crew without strain with any of the 'Deltics'.

As 1963 came to a close, it was reported that trials with Classes '40', '45', '46' and 'Deltics' were being conducted on the Leeds to Harrogate line, although the nature of these remained a mystery.

Also during 1963 it was decided that no 'Deltics' should be scheduled for overhaul during the summer timetables. This raised a difficulty in that the engine overhaul period at that time was 4,000 engine hours, and some units had to be sent to the works before this had elapsed to ensure that they were free of works' calls for the 1964 summer period. After this, modifications were carried out which enabled these intervals between overhauls to be extended to 6,000 hours.

1964

'...the average service reliability reached a very creditable figure of 97.9 per cent.'

By early 1964, 12 'Deltics' had been modified to run for 6,000 engine hours between overhauls and, by the summer timetable's commencement, 75 per cent of the class had been treated. Ultimately, a target of 8,000 engine hours was aimed at (about two years' service) and two 'Deltics' were used in 1964 in the initial experiments. Also by this time, with the almost total elimination of their 'bugs', the 'Deltics' became one of the undoubted successes of the modernization programme, 3.7 million miles having been covered by the 22 locomotives from August 1962 to August 1963.

During April, it was noted that Class '47' diesels were covering 'Deltic' diagrams due to some 'Deltics' being in Doncaster Works receiving their pre-summer service works overhaul. At the end of April, Eastern Region began a service of high-speed brake tests between Horn-

The fibreglass 'winged-thistle' headboard introduced to the 'Flying Scotsman' service during 1964 (H. Watson).

sey and Doncaster with a 'Deltic'-hauled 11-coach train, including a dynamometer car, for which the Civil Engineer had authorized speeds up to 105 mph.

During the year the 'Flying Scotsman' train service received new fibreglass headboards in the shape of a winged thistle. D9006 left Edinburgh adorned with this headboard on its inaugural southbound run. It is worth noting that by this time, the 'A4' 'Pacifics' had long since been banished to Scotland, although a few 'A3' 'Pacifics' were still scattered about the East Coast Main Line working freight, parcels and standby passenger duties, along with a few Peppercorn 'A1' 'Pacifics'. Such was the scene on Saturday 4 April when I well remember 'A1' 'Pacific' No 60124 *Kenilworth* standing adjacent to the turntable at Darlington Shed in pristine condition on standby duty, as 'Deltics' D9002/3/5/7/14 and 19 all sped by, none of them needing her help. Meanwhile, a couple of miles away in North Road Works, BR were breaking up 'Pacifics' Nos 60011 *Empire of India*, 60020 *Guillemot*, 60160 *Auld Reekie* and repairing 60133 *Pommern* and 60004 *William Whitelaw*. Later that day came the sight of No 4472 *Flying Scotsman* standing next to No 60045 *Lemberg* on Darlington Shed as D9005 flashed by in the distance.

On 20-21 April, the 'Deltics' were discussed at a meeting of the Institute of Mechanical Engineers. The report put forward was a refreshingly candid account of the troubles and defects encountered with the engines and the design changes introduced to overcome them. The first production 'Deltic' had begun East Coast Main Line service in March 1961, and during their first year at work the manufacturers

Gresley 'A3' 60036 Colombo *on stand-by duties at Darlington MPD* (N. Skinner).

learned the lesson that development tests of a full production standard engine should be completed in time for any necessary production modifications to take place. In this case they were not, and the early production 'Deltics' entered service or were delivered for installation before results had been reported and action decided.

Experience gained during that first year and remedial action taken encouraged the engineers to hope that further troubles would be confined to the pistons and cylinder liners. These had proved fallible to corrosion fatigue and development work to eradicate the causes was still in progress in 1964. In the event, there was only one other unexpected crop of troubles — a succession of coolant pump drive failures on several units. As a result, this item was re-designed.

During their second year in service, the 'Deltics' had achieved an average of 97 per cent of their gross possible running hours. This increased reliability, coupled with the ability to replace a defective engine in a locomotive in eight hours, meant that the average service reliability reached a very creditable figure of 97.9 per cent.

From October 1963, overhauled engines had been given strengthened cylinder liners, improved Mk 3 pistons and detail design improvements to the fuel pump idler gear bushes and exciter drive bearings. With the agreement of BR, four nominated engines were left in service for 8,000 hours to gain the necessary experience from engine-overhaul strip examinations to justify further extensions of the 'Deltic' overhaul life. The target interval, after Mk 4 pistons of improved design were fitted in 1965-66, became 10,000 hours between overhauls. At this point is should be noted that there were no minor or major partial overhauls on the 'Deltics' while the engine was in situ.

On 25 April, the East Coast Main Line was blocked at Belford in Northumberland, so causing 'Deltics' to appear at Carlisle via the Newcastle-Hexham-Carlisle route. One such was D9019 heading the 'Flying Scotsman', which arrived in Carlisle after taking the Waverley route from Edinburgh. Among other unusual routes to be used around this time by the 'Deltics' was the Perth to Inverness main line taken by D9004 on 22 May to gain access to the Highland capital on the occasion of its naming ceremony. Having travelled north on the night of 22-23 May with the sleeper from Edinburgh, D9004 was named *Queen's Own Highlander* and then returned south with the 17.45 'Royal Highlander' as far as Perth, thus becoming the first 'Deltic' to reach Inverness.

On the advent of the 1964 summer timetable, modest accelerations were made by reduction in recovery allowances for engineering work on all the King's Cross to Leeds, Newcastle and Edinburgh trains. On 15 June, both train sets of the 'Talisman' service were re-equipped for the summer timetable; the down afternoon train was formed of the new project XP64 stock, headed by an absolutely immaculate D9012 *Crepello*, and the down morning train had first class Pullman cars towards the rear of the formation and was headed by D9008 *The Green Howards*.

July saw the naming of yet another Haymarket-based 'Deltic', this

The massive bulk of a Napier 'Deltic' engine, one of two fitted inside each locomotive (S. Cholmondeley).

time D9016, which was named *Gordon Highlander* on 28 July at a ceremony at Aberdeen Station, which also featured the restored GNSR steam locomotive No 49 *Gordon Highlander*.

During August, Cecil J. Allen had the privilege of a run in the cab of D9016 *Gordon Highlander* on the southbound 'Flying Scotsman'. The train was an 11-coach formation of all but 400 tons tare, so affording the opportunity to see one of these powerful units on a fairly hard assignment. The run began to be logged after D9016 had arrived at Newcastle Central several minutes early, and where waiting passengers filled the train to capacity, making the 396 tons tare up to a gross weight of 425 tons. D9016 left Newcastle to the dead second at 11.58 and slid gently away on to the King Edward Bridge, round the further sharp curve at its south end, and then opened out. This, however, did not last long, for through Chester-le-Street there was a permanent way relaying slack that seemed almost endless — it meant 15 mph for a full mile — and this lost D9016 a full 6 minutes.

As compared with the days of pre-war streamliners, when the timings south of York were considerbly more exacting than those north of that point, today the opposite is the case. If speed restrictions are fully observed, a scheduled average speed such as the 89.5 mph from Nor-

thallerton to Skelton box — 28.35 miles in 19 mins — leaves no margin whatever for recovering lost time, and 2 mins only for the 1.6 miles round the curves to the centre of York Station is a virtual impossibility. So, despite the 3 mins recovery allowance from Ferryhill to Darlington, D9016 had picked up only 2 minutes of the lost time on passing York. Features on this stretch were a recovery from 30 to 47 mph up the 1 in 101 from Durham to Relly Mill, a 70 mph restriction that was then in force at Browney Colliery, Croxdale, and the more severe one over Aycliffe curve.

Through Darlington, D9016 provided some lively sensations at the full permitted 80 mph, then the restriction to this figure as far as Eryholme was faithfully observed. The then-90 mph maximum along the perfect racing stretch from Darlington to York was also meticulously kept to — indeed, for the most part to slightly under rather than over the prescribed figure — and, as a witness to the power that D9016 had in reserve, it was noted that round about Alne this 425-ton train was being raced along level track at 90 mph with the controller only half open and an amperage of no more than 800 reaching the traction motors.

After York there were easings over Chaloners Whin Junction and Naburn swingbridge, and the Escrick signalman was slow in pulling off,

causing a half-minute loss. Selby then demanded a long slack, from
60 mph round the curve at Barlby to 40 mph over the swingbridge. The
reason for the slight slack at Balne was not noted, but it mattered little as,
with the help of a second 3 min recovery, D9016 was dead on time
through Doncaster. The 60 mph restriction through Doncaster then in
force extended to beyond Black Carr Junction, and with the long-
continued slowing over Bawtry Viaduct there was little chance of
making any speed until beyond Retford, which made matters worse by
slowing D9016 down to 33 mph for signals.

Up the grade from Retford to Markham, *Gordon Highlander*
accelerated to 74 mph and then, after a brief 86 mph, there followed the
usual easing down the 1 in 200 to Crow Park and the slack then in force
for Muskham water troughs. Despite all these delays, D9016 was still
sticking closely to schedule times. The controller was now moved to the
fully open position and this resulted in a steady 86-84 mph up the 1 in
200 to Peascliffe Tunnel on 1,300 amps and, while fully open after the
70 mph Grantham slack, produced an acceleration to 77.5 mph up the
similar grade to Stoke Summit, the dial here showing 1,500 amps. It
may be added that the first transition to weak field on a 'Deltic' takes
place at about 50 mph and the second around 75 mph, with a perceptible
drop in engine noise as each change takes place; automatic controls
quickly restore the normal 1,500 rpm engine speed.

Once over Stoke Summit, D9016 accelerated in lightning fashion
in 3 miles to Corby Glen, where speed had climbed from 77.5 to
96 mph, and a little over a mile later the 100 mph mark was reached (the
actual maximum was 102.5 mph). Unhappily, permanent way relaying
work was in progress at Essendine and the speed had to come down from
three figures to 20 mph; even so, D9016 succeeded in accelerating back
to 92 mph before having to reduce to 60 mph for Werrington water
troughs, where D9016 was still dead on time. After Peterborough a little
too much respect was paid to Stilton Fen, with a reduction to 65 mph at
Holme. Up the 1 in 200 from Conington there was a slight acceleration
from 82 to 83.5 mph, and then came yet another permanent way
relaying slack of 20 mph at Stukeley before Huntingdon.

Sandy was passed on time to the dead second, but D9016 was then
slowed to 46 mph by signals when approaching Hitchin and to 20 mph
for the fifth engineering slack, through Stevenage Station, while signals
yet again caused delay at Welwyn Garden City. With full use of the
relaxed limit to 80 mph through Wood Green, notwithstanding the five
severe permanent way slowings and four signal checks of varying
severity, D9016 was still on time through Finsbury Park and all set for a
punctual arrival — but no! A 'double yellow' at Holloway heralded a
dead stand for signals at Belle Isle. And why? To allow the empty
coaches of the 09.00 from Edinburgh to pass out of King's Cross straight
across D9016's path! As a result of this maddening check, for which
there could have been little excuse, D9016 came to a stand in King's
Cross 2.5 minutes late.

Running at such high speeds for long distances with such regularity was the hallmark of the 'Deltics'. One might have thought that this would give them more chance of being involved in accidents than other classes of diesels, but this was not so, for they earned a good reputation for accident-free mileage. However, one such accident in which a 'Deltic' was involved was on 28 October when D9007 *Pinza* was badly damaged at the leading end in a collision with a derailed freight train near Selby while working the down 'Heart of Midlothian'. The freight train included in its formation a number of petrol wagons and it was fortunate that they were empty. D9007 was removed to Doncaster Works after the incident.

The end of the year saw the naming of another of Haymarket's 'Deltics'; D9006 was named *The Fife and Forfar Yeomanry* at a ceremony at Cupar Station on 5 December.

1965

'...for the first time in railway history, the scheduled service time from King's Cross to Edinburgh dropped below six hours...'

D9014 The Duke of Wellington's Regiment *drifts into Darlington past Parkgate Junction with a morning Newcastle to King's Cross service* (D. Carter).

From 9 January 1965, another section of the East Coast Main Line, the 21 miles from Cadwell to Offord, was passed for 100 mph running, bringing the total 100 mph mileage on this route to just over 51. Another 42 miles between Skelton Junction, York and Darlington were passed for speeds of up to 95 mph. These lengths gave the 'Deltics' even more chance to show their paces and time recovery capabilities.

On 5 January, D9014 put up an excellent performance with the 08.00 Edinburgh to King's Cross which, as a result of a derailment at Selby, was diverted via Knottingley. The train passed Doncaster 20 mins late, but with a time of 119 mins for the 156 miles from Don-

caster to King's Cross, an average speed of 78 mph was attained, and arrival was on time.

Cecil J. Allen recorded another run during this period on the up 'Tees-Tyne Pullman', which was hauled by an unidentified 'Deltic'. On the particular Monday morning in question, the train was not merely made up to 8 coaches (one over the normal complement), but a bogie brake was also attached, making the total load up to 360 tons tare and about 375 tons gross. The train got away to a 19-mins late start from Newcastle due to the fact that the Gateshead Depot staff had been having trouble with the steam heating boiler of this particular locomotive. From the start it soon became clear that the London driver had every intention of making up the arrears of time; as early as Birtley, speed was up to 88 mph, and after the Durham slack and the 70 mph imposed at Browney Colliery, the train reached 90 mph before slowing for the Aycliffe curve. Notwithstanding adverse signals at the approach to Darlington, 5 minutes were regained over this initial stretch and, by smart station working at Bank Top recouping nearly another minute, the train restarted from Darlington 13.25 mins late only. On the second fastest British scheduled run at that time there was some lively running, with the top speed just reaching 100 mph on the dead level at Alne, with the result that the 44.1 miles from Darlington to York, including the 72 mph slack over Wiske Moor troughs, were run in 33 mins 48 secs start-to-stop. York Station staff also handled the train expeditiously, and the non-stop-run for King's Cross began only 11.5 mins behind time.

Soon after leaving York, the train suffered a bad relaying check to 20 mph at Escrick and then, after 95.5 mph had been reached at Balne, the 'Deltic' received some unkind treatment through Doncaster, signal checks from Shaftsholme Junction culminating in a near dead stand at Arksey. Thus, notwithstanding the 3 mins recovery allowance between Selby and Shaftsholme, 3.5 mins were dropped from York to Doncaster. There was a fine acceleration from 66 mph through Retford to 82 mph up the 1 in 178-200 to Markham Summit. After this, despite a 25 mph permanent way slack at Retford and a signal check beyond Claypole, some hard uphill running with speed maintained at 82 mph up the 1 in 200 to Stoke Summit, resulted in the 'Deltic' passing Stoke box having recovered all the time lost since leaving York.

Now followed a most rousing descent of Stoke Bank, with an average of 103.4 mph maintained over the 15.25 miles from Stoke to Tallington, and a top speed of 105 mph. By Peterborough all but 10 minutes of the train's late start had been recovered, despite the delays the 'Deltic' had suffered to this point. However, the most brilliant running still lay ahead. Up the 4.5 miles of 1 in 200 past Abbots Ripton the train forged its way without speed falling below 90 mph; a brief 95 mph through Huntingdon preceded the 72 mph Offord curve slowing. Between 88 and 90 mph was sustained from St Neots to Biggleswade, and Sandy was passed with the 'Pullman' now no more than 2 minutes behind time. Through Three Counties the 'Deltic' was doing 94 mph, but just when the train had a certain prospect of passing Hitchin ahead of time, it was almost all but stopped by an irritating signal check at Cadwell. Nothing daunted, the 'Deltic' accelerated up the 1 in 200 to 72 mph before reaching the summit at Stevenage; then followed 90 mph by Knebworth and 94 mph before yet another severe slack for relaying before Hatfield.

After this the proceedings became exciting indeed as, with a somewhat liberal interpretation of the speed rubrics, the 'Deltic' then touched 95 mph through Hadley Wood and continued at well over 80 mph until slowed at Wood Green Tunnel. It is astonishing to relate that after the 19 mins late start and delays which between them had cost fully 16 mins (1 min Darlington; 2 mins Escrick; 5.25 mins Shaftsholme, Doncaster; 2 mins Newark; 0.5 min Hougham; 3.5 mins Cadwell; and 1.75 mins Welwyn Garden City), the train swept through Finsbury Park 2 mins early — and then (need it be said?) a dead stand of just over 2 mins at Belle Isle and an arrival in King's Cross all but 4 mins late! What a discouraging trick to play on a keen driver, and one which seems to happen all too often.

By February, work had started on fitting the 'Deltics' with cast steel bogie frames in an attempt to overcome the tendency of the original type to fracture. These frames were interchangeable with the Class '37's. Meanwhile, D9012 had its controls modified to reduce wheel–slip troubles, and the remainder of the class was expected to be dealt with similarly.

By April, the intensive rostering of the 'Deltics' working the fastest trains in Britain at that time showed that during the 12 weeks from 15 June to September 1964, the 'Deltics' had been scheduled to run 1,147,908 miles, and actually achieved 1,042,685 miles, indicating an availability of over 90 per cent. When it is remembered that a major pro-portion of the 105,223 miles lost had probably been caused by cir-cumstances other than mechanical or electrical failure, the record becomes even better. Extrapolation indicates that if service throughout the year had been maintained at summer peak level (which it obviously was not), the actual diagram mileage for the year would be about 4.3 million. An equivalent diagram mileage for the year would be about 4.9 million, or 225,000 miles per 'Deltic' annually, more than the mileage envisaged for the locomotives when they were ordered.

The first fruits of the increase in the maximum permitted speed to 100 mph over certain parts of the East Coast Main Line were to be seen in the summer timetable of 1965. The most interesting outcome was that for the first time in railway history, the scheduled service time from King's Cross to Edinburgh and vice versa dropped below six hours. The 'Deltic'-hauled 'Flying Scotsman' made the 392.8-mile journey in 5 hrs 55 mins, including the Newcastle stop. More notable was the accelera-tion of the morning 'Talisman'. As experience proved, the up afternoon 'Talisman' easily completed the journey from Edinburgh to London in six hours with stops at Newcastle, Darlington and Hitchin. The morn-ing train, the 08.00 from Edinburgh, was accelerated by 15 mins to reach King's Cross at 14.00 with stops at Berwick, Newcastle and Darl-

D9003 Meld *at speed on the down morning King's Cross to Glasgow train between the tunnels at Welwyn* (D. Carter Collection)

ington. The down morning 'Talisman', the 08.00 from King's Cross, however, had five stops and was allowed $6\frac{1}{4}$ hrs to Edinburgh. Most of the other East Coast Main Line trains were also accelerated by 5 mins by virtue of this 100 mph authorization. In fact, by the commencement of the summer 1965 timetable, the East Coast Main Line had about 125 route miles where three-figure speeds could be reached.

Nonetheless, even in 1965 'Deltics' were, at times, to be seen on menial duties, as was witnessed on 10 March with the use of D9020 *Nimbus* on the 17.05 Baldock to King's Cross.

Among other 'Deltic' activities during early 1965 was the naming of D9010 *The King's Own Scottish Borderer* at a special ceremony at Dumfries on 8 May. After the ceremony, D9010 left Dumfries on a special train carrying territorials of the King's Own Scottish Borderers to their annual camp, which it worked as far as Perth.

During June, D9018 *Ballymoss* was noted fitted with air-horns mounted on the top corners of the nose-casing in front of the windscreen, which was to become the standard fitting place for the whole class, albeit some years later, instead of underneath the buffer-beam or on the top of the cab-roof ends, which position was unique to D9019, D9020, D9021 and the prototype unit.

By mid-summer 1965, the demise of steam was well advanced with quite a few classes now totally extinct, and Darlington scrapyard was thriving on ripping apart these now miserable-looking hulks. However, on the brighter side one such locomotive was noted on the 'dead line' at Darlington Shed on 15 July – it was 'A4' 'Pacific' No 60010 *Dominion of Canada*, which, happily, is now preserved in that country, although on that day she was standing almost adjacent to the main line, forlorn, minus chimney, nameplates and most of her former dignity, awaiting entry into North Road Works. It was from this spot that, in the space of half an hour, I noted 'Deltics' D9001 and D9006 as they sped by with interested passengers passing a quick eye over this now-happily resurrected locomotive.

August was a month of pleasant weather, and on 11 July I cycled to Bradbury on the East Coast Main Line. On that day predominating classes were '40's, '46's, '47's and '24's, then allocated to Gateshead and Thornaby Depots. That day saw only one steam engine, 'V2' No 60806 heading south light engine. By this time the 'Deltics' had been running for four years and were well in command — units noted on that particular day were D9006/10/2/16/8 and D9000, in that order.

The attempt to use all 22 'Deltics' throughout the 1965 summer service did not work out in practice, for at least three of the London units were in Doncaster Works in mid-August. As a result, Classes '40' and '47' were employed as occasional 'Deltic' substitutes, with consequent timekeeping difficulties. To expect a 100 per cent turnout during that period would have been very optimistic with any class of locomotive and was asking for trouble, even considering that all the 'Deltics' had received their pre-summer overhauls and checks.

Towards the close of the year, the daily 'Deltic' average mileage

Withdrawn, but certainly not life expired, redundant Peppercorn 'A1' 60158 Aberdonian *stands on the 'dead-line' at Darlington MPD awaiting her call to the scrapyard during February 1965 (N. Skinner).*

achieved was 433. As a result, more than half of the 'Deltic' fleet had an availability record of over 80 per cent up to a maximum, in two cases, of 86.8 per cent, though none quite reached 90.5 per cent, the availability quoted by the manufacturers. In fact, the lowest figure was 72.7 per cent. D9013 had an astonishing record of maintaining an average speed of 62.1 mph over 166,334 miles of travel, and D9004 of 60.4 mph over 184,160 miles.

In the 12 months from August 1961, the 'Deltics' had amassed a total of 2,750,000 miles. In the ensuing twelve months the figure had risen to 3,669,820 miles. From mid-August 1963 to the end of 1964, the figure had climbed to 5,125,000 miles, which was a rate of 170,000 miles a year per unit. On these performances it was quite probable, at that time, that some of the 'Deltics' could have achieved the guaranteed 220,000 miles (665 miles per day over 331 days in the year) if sufficient high-speed duties at suitable times had been arranged. After all, each 'Deltic' doing the round King's Cross-Edinburgh trip in 24 hours covered 786 miles, but this was not, of course, possible on the King's Cross-Leeds service.

September saw the last un-named 'Deltic', D9019, named *Royal Highland Fusilier* at a ceremony in Glasgow on the 11th, so at the end of 1965 all the 'Deltics' had received names.

The nameplate and regimental crest of D9019 Royal Highland Fusilier *(S. Cholmondeley).*

1966

'The excitement started when the summer timetable was announced...'

The down 'Flying Scotsman' accelerates away from York behind D9020 Nimbus (D. Carter Collection).

During early 1966, the maintenance contract between British Rail and English Electric for the maintenance of the 22 'Deltics' expired. Thereafter the units were cared for totally by British Railways, who did a grand job to ensure that the maintenance level of these unique locomotives did not drop.

The first few months of the year slipped by without very much happening on the 'Deltic' scene, with the whole class going about their duties without incident. The excitement started when the summer timetable was announced and again introduced still more cuts in journey times. The morning 'Talisman' added York to its Hitchin, Grantham, Darlington, Newcastle and Berwick stops, yet still reached Edinburgh in 6¼ hours. The 'Flying Scotsman' ran to Newcastle in, up until then, the fastest time ever, 3 hrs 53 mins, and on to Edinburgh in 5 hrs 50 mins. The afternoon 'Talisman' made the non–stop run from

King's Cross to Darlington in 3 hrs 18 mins, the same time as the pre-war 'Silver Jubilee', but with a tare load of 385 tons, compared with the 248 tons of the 'Jubilee', and with various speed restrictions which were not enforced in the 1935-39 period. The effect of these accelerations was that the ten day trains between King's Cross and Edinburgh, five in each direction, averaged 6 hrs 13 mins over the 393 miles at a mean speed of 63 mph, including a total of 41 stops. Newcastle had the use of 22 day trains in all, to and from London, with a combined average time of 4 hrs 20 mins for the 268.3 miles, an average speed of 61. 9 mph.

Meanwhile, Leeds was treated to its fastest journey times ever, with times such as 3 hrs 5 mins, 2 hrs 56 mins and 3 hrs 23 mins, depending on what stops each particular service made. On all the fastest services the 'Deltics', with 385 tons or 11 coaches, were allowed the following times:

To Peterborough:	64 mins	(76 miles)
To Grantham:	87 mins	(105.5 miles)
To Doncaster:	133.5 mins	(156 miles)
To York:	161.5 mins	(188.2 miles)
To Darlington:	196 mins	(232.3 miles)
To Newcastle:	233 mins	(268.3 miles)

All the above were passing times — one minute more was allowed for a stop.

It was during the currency of the 1966 summer timetable that the East Coast Main Line's first 'Deltic'-hauled 80 mph run became a reality with the 'Tees-Tyne Pullman' from Darlington to York, 44.1 miles in 33 mins at 80.2 mph. A number of 455-ton trains also covered this stretch in 35 mins at 75.6 mph start-to-stop. In fact, this timetable showed that the Eastern Region's point-to-point bookings were faster than the London Midland's electric services, and up to that time, faster than anywhere else in Europe. The showpieces were the new 2 hrs 40 mins Leeds flyers, with an average speed of 91.6 mph for the 11.45 miles from Essendine up to Stoke Summit, almost entirely uphill at 1 in 200 and 178, with a 'Deltic'-hauled 8-coach 286-ton tare load. In fact, in July's railway press it was stated that railway records were being broken, leaving the accustomed observer breathless with such happenings as a 'Deltic' having to be braked from 96 mph up to Stoke Summit in order to come down to the 90 mph speed limit!

During 1966, Cecil J. Allen wrote of a run behind D9001 *St Paddy,* which proved just how much the 'Deltics' always had in hand when required. The run in question was the 07.55 'North Eastern' from Newcastle to King's Cross. On that day, the 11-coach train of 394 tons, laid down as the maximum for this timing, had no fewer than five additional coaches attached for a special party, bringing the tare weight up to 565 tons — by far the maximum Mr Allen had ever known on one of these high-speed timings. Despite this massive train, *St Paddy* was to at-

After its high-speed sprint from Darlington, the up 'Tees-Tyne Pullman' stands at York behind D9005 The Prince of Wales's Own Regiment of Yorkshire (D. Carter).

tempt to work from Darlington to King's Cross at an average of 70.4 mph, in other words in the same 198 mins as the pre-war 'Silver Jubilee', a train of a mere 220 tare tons in its earlier days. *St Paddy* not only succeeded in keeping time, but also achieved a net time of 191.75 mins for the 232.15 miles, a gain of 6.25 mins on schedule.

Over the level stretch from Darlington to York, the weight of the train naturally had its effect on performance and, despite the attainment of 94 mph on the slight descents past Otterington and Pilmoor, 2.5 mins were lost on the sharp booked time to Skelton. Signal checks through York then added to the loss which by Selby had mounted to 6.5 mins. Through Doncaster a clear road was obtained, though even with the help of 5 mins recovery time the arrears had not been reduced to less than 4.5 mins by Retford, and a signal check made the 'North Eastern' once again 6.5 mins late past Newark.

St. Paddy now demonstrated its ability to sustain 70.5-71 mph with this 600-ton gross train up a gradient of 1 in 200, for this was the minimum at both Peascliffe Tunnel and Stoke Summit. Down the racing ground from Stoke, 96 mph was touched at two points (Little Bytham and Tallington) and, despite another signal check, Peterborough was passed no more than 6 mins behind time. South of Peterborough, *St Paddy* worked magnificently. With a clear road throughout, the whole of the arrears were recovered and *St Paddy* swept through Finsbury Park just ahead of time.

It was true that the gain of 6.5 mins from Peterborough to Finsbury Park was balanced by 6 mins recovery time in the schedule, but even so one or two extraordinary feats were performed and none more so than to complete the climb to Stevenage at 78.5 mph. After Three Counties this was first 1.25 miles at 1 in 264 and then 5 miles continuously at 1 in 200; from Three Counties up to Stevenage the average speed was 83.6 mph and the total drop in speed no more than from 89 to 78.5 mph. Up this short stretch, the power output must have been appreciably in excess of the one hour 3,300 hp rating of a 'Deltic'. Finally, there was the not unusual experience of signal obstruction at Belle Isle, but happily not severe, and the run ended with an excess of no more than 1.25 mins over schedule time; as previously mentioned, the net time was 6.25 mins less than that scheduled. I doubt if there has ever been a finer 'Deltic' effort than this.

from a number of their diagrams, presumably because of scheduled overhaul requirements, thus throwing out the timekeeping when Class '40's and '47's had to stand in, although 40081 turned up at King's Cross 3 mins early on the 'Yorkshire Pullman'. One 'Deltic' that passed through the works at this time was D9002 *The King's Own Yorkshire Light Infantry,* which during October was the first 'Deltic' to appear in the 'rail-blue' livery with all-over yellow ends. Among the more unusual 'Deltic' turns was on 5 November when an unidentified unit deputized for a DMU on the 08.34 Corstorphine to Edinburgh Waverley, hauling a 6-coach train!

So 1966 went out in a big way for the 'Deltics', which continued to amaze the enthusiast with their record-breaking qualities, and it also was the beginning of their era in the rail-blue livery. However, it should not be forgotten that these standards were very hard to keep up from the maintenance point of view, and were achieved only by the high maintenance standards set for these machines. Of course, things did go wrong from time to time during the year; one such day was 17 February when both D9002 and D9001 failed at Peterborough North Station heading Newcastle and Leeds trains respectively.

1967

'Several of the fleet had exceeded individual totals of 1 million miles.'

Further progress in the provision of fast, frequent runs was made from 6 March 1967. Journey times from London were now: 230 mins to Newcastle, 190 mins to Darlington, 165 mins to York and 189 mins to Hull. Between Leeds and London, the high-speed service times varied between 2 hrs 42 mins and 2 hrs 48 mins. One area of note was the York to Darlington racing stretch, which was not quite as fast as the previous year's timetable. Apart from the 'Tees-Tyne Pullman', about half of the trains had a minute added to their schedules. Even the up 'Flying Scotsman' had its pass-to-pass time extended by $\frac{1}{2}$ minute.

On 10 May things were not going too well for D9016 *Gordon Highlander* which failed heading the 11.00 Newcastle to King's Cross. It was noticed being towed into York by Class '47' No D1986, complete with train, running 15 mins late. D9016 was quickly removed to York Motive Power Depot and was seen later that day being towed away to Doncaster Works for repairs to one of its engines.

At about this time, steam was all but finished in the Teesside area, and for the first and only time in my life I almost decided to give up train-spotting! Class '37's had replaced my beloved 'Q6's, 'J27's and 'B1's, and it seemed that the rot had set in when, during the year, I acquired a driving licence and my world expanded overnight. More frequent visits to the East Coast Main Line became possible, and it was there, at last, that the 'Deltic's really took over from the 'A3' and 'A4' 'Pacifics' in my affections.

A special moment in the life of D9005 occurred on 17 June when it was rostered to haul the return leg of the 'Hadrian Flyer' from Carlisle over Aisgill Summit to Leeds, Doncaster and King's Cross. Throughout the trip, D9005 was reported by O.S Nock to have performed most admirably, taking Aisgill in its stride with its 365 tons gross load, and really flying once the East Coast Main Line was gained at Doncaster. A time of 132 mins for the non-stop run of 156 miles from Doncaster to King's Cross was scheduled, which involved an average speed of 71 mph and which, with the restrictions of the road and two in-

Although taken during 1963, this photograph highlights the anguish of the railway enthusiast during the transition period — harmless little 'J72' 68723 comes alongside the bulk of D9005 on the up 'Talisman' at Newcastle Central (H. Watson).

cidental checks, left little margin in reserve. D9005, however, sustained uphill speeds of around 80 mph on the various 1 in 200 ascents. In the overall average speed, one notices particularly the effect of a succession of small hindrances — 45 mph at Bawtry Viaduct; 60 mph at Retford; 60 mph at Markham troughs; 70 mph at Grantham; the Offord curves; and finally the 80 mph limit then prevailing from Hatfield inwards.

On the basis of the general performance of D9005, Mr Nock estimated the cost of the Hitchin signal check at 2.5 mins and that of the New Southgate permanent way check at 2.25 mins, thus leaving an overall net time of 125.5 mins and a 74.7 mph average speed. Quite apart from the usual 100 mph descending from Stoke to Peterborough, D9005 sustained that speed on level track between Tempsford and Biggleswade, where the average speed was 101 mph over 6.3 miles. Another very fine performance was the recovery from Muskham slack up the rising gradient towards Peascliffe Tunnel, when speed reached 97 mph between Claypole and Hougham and had not fallen below 92 mph at Barkston. It was a pity that the regulation slack at Grantham supervened, because on gradients alone D9005 might have been doing nearly 100 mph there and cleared Stoke Summit at over 90 mph. Once over Stoke, D9005 maintained speeds of 100 mph and over onwards to Essendine, before easing down for the Peterborough slack, and eventually reached King's Cross in 130 mins 20 secs — a fine performance!

D9001 *St Paddy* was noted on 6 August working the 05.50 Doncaster to Hull train. At that time it was unusual to see this loco at Hull and it presumably worked away on the 09.30 return train to King's Cross.

In September it was announced that the 22 locomotives had travelled a combined total of 21 million miles in 5.5 years. This represented an average of 500 miles per day throughout this period for each unit.

D9000 Royal Scots Grey *rolls into York on the down morning King's Cross to Glasgow train* (J. W. Armstrong).

Several of the fleet had also, by this time, exceeded individual totals of 1 million miles.

The latter part of the year passed without incident, units making their appearances at Doncaster Works for the usual repairs and examinations and, in general, going about their everyday tasks with the utmost reliability.

1968

'...the 40th anniversary of non-stop running between London and Edinburgh...'

During the latter half of January, the 'Deltics' began to be used occasionally on Edinburgh to Aberdeen trains. D9004 *Queen's Own Highlander* passed through Cupar travelling north at 12.30 on 3 February; apparently the locomotive and coaches were undergoing speed and braking trials, and there were no passengers on board. Later the same day, D9010 *The King's Own Scottish Borderer* passed by heading the 19.59 Aberdeen to Edinburgh train.

In March, D9009 *Alycidon* was at Doncaster Works undergoing extensive repairs following severe fire damage. This near catastrophe happened when *Alycidon* was temporarily re-allocated to Edinburgh Haymarket Depot for a period of six months in 1967 whilst her Haymarket sisters were undergoing the fitting of air-brake equipment at Doncaster Works. This fire was, in fact, the worst that any 'Deltic' suffered and, once released from the works in the new rail-blue livery, it returned to Finsbury Park Depot in June.

D9005 The Prince of Wales's own Regiment of Yorkshire *at Darlington on the down 'Aberdonian'* (D. Allinson).

During the same month, D9007 *Pinza* was noted off the beaten track. On 8 March it was seen heading a train from King's Cross to Leeds diverted via Featherstone, where it was noted at 14.28. D9007 was also by this time displaying the all rail-blue livery with enlarged yellow ends.

On 1 May, to celebrate the 40th anniversary of non-stop running between London and Edinburgh, Class 'A3' 'Pacific' No 4472 *Flying Scotsman* left King's Cross on a special steam run non-stop to Edinburgh, whilst D9021 *Argyll and Sutherland Highlander* departed simultaneously from the adjacent platform with the present-day 'Flying Scotsman' train. D9021, with a Newcastle stop, reached Edinburgh nearly two hours earlier than No 4472.

After *Flying Scotsman's* heavily publicized run it seemed only fair that a 'Deltic' should get a little limelight; on 4 May D9020 *Nimbus* was chosen to work the Locomotive Club of Great Britain's hired train from King's Cross to Edinburgh, named 'The East Coast Limited'.

A visit to Gateshead MPD the following day proved that the 'Deltics' were in demand even on Sundays, as the only two 'Deltics' on shed were D9011 *The Royal Northumberland Fusilier* and a visitor, D9007 *Pinza,* standing at the fuelling stage. Nearby, among the Class '24's, '37's and '47's, were some of the ill-fated Class '17's (or 'Claytons'), D8591 and D8594, at that time allocated to Gateshead.

On 16 June, I was in York roundhouse, now part of the National Railway Museum, admiring 'A4' No 60019 *Bittern,* then awaiting preservation, when outside D9014 *The Duke of Wellington's Regiment* thundered north out of the station, cascading exhaust everywhere and emitting that famous vociferous roar — a 'Deltic' in true form! Mention of these locomotives in full cry appropriately introduces a run, witnessed by O. S. Nock behind D9018 *Ballymoss* heading the northbound 'Flying Scotsman' during 1968. On the more northerly stretches there was a very strong crosswind which prevented *Ballymoss* from attaining the level 100 mph near Thirsk. Mr Nock formed the impression that with the then present speed limits and loading there was not a great deal of time to spare on that schedule with a 'Deltic'. But D9018 was dead on time through Hitchin and made the customary 100 mph sprint onwards to St Neots with an average speed of 101 mph over this 19.8 miles stretch, and a maximum of 104 mph.

During June, the 'Deltics' were not only showing their prowess on high-speed expresses, but also their ability at times of pressure on the loco departments to haul more menial trains. On 8 June, for example, D9003 *Meld* turned its hand to working a morning parcels train from Edinburgh to Dundee. On the other side of the coin, however, the 'Deltics' could still, when the fancy took them, fail at the most inconvenient times, such as D9014 on 22 July which, whilst working the 16.00 King's Cross-Edinburgh, failed at Doncaster and was quickly replaced by Class '47' D1783 for the remainder of the journey north. On the 28th of that month, D9010 suffered a fire in one of its cabs and was later noted in Doncaster Works.

Sporting the rather ungainly-looking all-over yellow end combined with the two-tone green livery, D9006 The Fife and Forfar Yeomanry speeds past Bradbury, Co Durham, on an up morning Newcastle to King's Cross service, 15 June 1968 (D. Carter).

Between October 1967 and July 1968, probably the two most important modifications to the 'Deltics' were carried out following the advent of the Mk II coach. This was the fitting of dual brakes and electric train heating. D9016 was the first to receive dual brakes on 7 October 1967, and all the 'Deltics' had been thus modified by 8 July 1968 when D9011 was converted.

The inaugural run of British Railways' new venture, the 'Euro-Scot Freightliner', took place on 7 October, headed by D9021 (complete with special headboard) which performed admirably. Although the 'Deltics' were not rostered to haul these freightliners, as time went by it was not unusual to find one being used on this type of train.

As was the case on many of the main lines of British Railways during 1968, improvements to the track both up and down the East Coast Main Line were taking place. Such was the case between Newcastle and Morpeth on 3 November, when all trains were diverted via the Blyth and Tyne freight lines, regaining the main line at Morpeth on the down road and Newcastle on the up. These diversions brought first-ever appearances of D9005, D9013 and D9019 to these lines, while further south on 30 September services between Wakefield and Doncaster had been diverted via Knottingley, bringing D9017 amongst other 'Deltics' to this route.

So, as 1968 came to a close and engineering works continued on the East Coast Main Line, bringing with them better riding conditions and improvements in speed, the 'Deltics' were ready to rise to even greater heights.

1969

'D9014 was the last 'Deltic' to retain the splendid two-tone green livery...'

Apart from normal diagram working, the 'Deltics' were now becoming popular for special workings. On 4 January, for example, D9002 *The King's Own Yorkshire Light Infantry* headed 'The Waverley' tour from Newcastle to Edinburgh via Riccarton Junction, returning via Berwick. The train comprised 11 well-filled coaches. Another unusual assignment befell D9018 *Ballymoss* on 22 January when it was chosen to work 1E-00 parcels diagram from Leeds via Doncaster to Sheffield Midland, later returning with 1D-20, the 04.30 parcels to Leeds.

North of the border, the frequent sight of 'Deltics' on the Edinburgh to Aberdeen services continued; D9000 *Royal Scots Grey,* for example, was at the head of the 12.30 Aberdeen to Edinburgh on 26 March. It had presumably worked north on a similar train earlier that day. Still in Scotland, on Tuesday 15 April, D9019 *Royal Highland Fusilier* unusually worked over the Highland main line for the first time. It was

Out on the Aberdeen road, a driver's-eye view from the cab of 9015 Tulyar *near Arbroath* (D. Carter).

noted piloting Type 2 D5338 on the Perth to Inverness mail train, and later that evening, returned south on a special troop train. Although these magnificent machines were thus spreading their wings still further, in the main they remained the stalwarts of the East Coast route, working their way into every train-spotter's heart from King's Cross to the far north of Scotland!

The 1969 summer timetable restored the 80 mph schedule of the 'Tees-Tyne Pullman' between York and Darlington after a three-year lapse. A sad note, however, was the transfer of the 'Master Cutler' (an ex-DP2 and 'Falcon' turn) over to the Midland route from Sheffield to St Pancras, ostensibly to give the path to a Hull train. Another development, which led to higher speeds between Darlington and Newcastle, was the appearance of the first mile-a-minute schedule between Durham and Darlington.

During June it was noted that the twin 'Napier' engines of the 'Deltics' were now being overhauled at Doncaster Works, that Doncaster staff had been trained at Liverpool and also that all future overhauls were undertaken in the Engine Repair Shop at Doncaster.

During their whole life, the 'Deltics' were always locomotives capable of almost anything in the way of high-speed haulage, yet during 1969 the high-speed trains between King's Cross and Leeds were running to a maximum booked load of 290 tons. The reason for this was that both up and down train schedules were timed right to the limit for the loads hauled, and the power of the 'Deltics' was needed for rapid acceleration after speed restrictions to attain as quickly as possible the maximum permitted speed on the succeeding section. Any hesitancy or leisureliness by the driver, and time would be lost, for these recovery margins built into the timetable provided virtually the only such opportunity.

The pace at which these trains ran is exemplified by the following run, recorded by O.S. Nock on the 11.30 King's Cross to Leeds, hauled by D9020 *Nimbus*. The 8-coach train was formed of air-braked stock, which was then standard on these services, and although the weather was beastly with a biting east wind and frequent snow showers, it in no way handicapped the running.

With a relatively light load for a 'Deltic', *Nimbus* made short work of Holloway Bank, but could not really get going until clear of the 60 mph limit north of Wood Green Tunnel. *Nimbus* then sailed in grand style up to Potters Bar and it was a novel experience to be, as Mr Nock put it, at 'less than even time' on passing the summit. From there until *Nimbus* was through Hitchin it was a question of running within speed limits and observing a temporary speed restriction to 60 mph at Stevenage. North of Hitchin, the speed limit was raised to 100 mph and from Three Counties to St Neots, *Nimbus* averaged 99.7 mph. This was nothing but the bare demands of this schedule, where the 27 miles from Hitchin to Huntingdon were allowed no more than 17 mins; in fact, *Nimbus* took only 16 mins 51 secs.

Onwards to Peterborough the going was easier, with 2 mins

recovery time, slow running across the fens in a heavy snowstorm and a very cautious approach to Peterborough itself. Recovering afterwards, D9020 had to be restrained until the then restricted length past Werrington was cleared, but by Tallington *Nimbus* was on to another 100 mph stretch and, despite frequent snow squalls, averaged 97 mph from Tallington to Corby. Just beyond Corby box, *Nimbus* was definitely eased so as not to enter the 90 mph section at Stoke Summit at excessive speed. Actually, the train came down to 77 mph but on this stretch had gained a little time, covering the Werrington to Stoke section in 13 mins 20 secs against the 14 mins scheduled.

At Grantham there was a heavy permanent way check to 30 mph and this absorbed most of the time *Nimbus* had in hand. From here onwards it was very much a case of running by fits and starts, with numerous slight speed restrictions, several signal checks and lots more snow. Retford was passed on time and, despite two more permanent way checks (the second near Rossington — a very long one), the 3 mins

In resplendent condition, 9010 The King's Own Scottish Borderer approaches Penmanshiel Tunnel on an up King's Cross working. (Note the mixed maroon and blue/grey coaching stock, a feature of that period).

recovery allowance enabled *Nimbus* to pass Doncaster Station on time. D9020 was, however, drawing in to a dead stand at the north end of the station and this was the prelude to a succession of checks that eventually made the train 9 mins late into Wakefield. A slower train had been allowed to precede the 11.30 from Doncaster and apparently continued up the bank in front of *Nimbus* to Ardsley but, with the aid of 3 mins recovery time, *Nimbus* managed to arrive in Leeds only 6 mins late.

As far as the ordinary running of 'Deltics' is concerned, another good run recorded by Mr Nock was behind D9010 *The King's Own Scottish Borderer* with a gross load of 460 tons on the 17.30 up from York. Despite an out-of-course stop because of a block failure at Grove Road Crossing just south of Retford, D9010 covered the 82.7 miles from York to Grantham in 78 mins 55 secs, with some 90 mph running on the level between Selby and Doncaster. From Grantham to Stoke box was covered in 6 mins 33 secs at 71 mph, the Corby-Tallington length was covered in 8 mins 3 secs with a maximum of 95 mph and Peterborough

was passed in 25 mins 28 secs. The Huntingdon-Hitchin length of 27 miles was covered in 18 mins 38 secs with a maximum speed of 93 mph, but the last stages were subject to a succession of checks, and the 31.9 miles from Hitchin into King's Cross took 33 mins 40 secs, the 73.6 miles from Grantham to Hitchin having been covered in 58 mins 53 secs. Even with the checks from Hitchin inwards, D9010 completed the 105.5 miles from Grantham to King's Cross in 92 mins 33 secs. The recovery power of the 'Deltics' resulted in checks having a far less serious effect on overall times than with the less powerful locomotives, both diesel and steam, which preceded them.

Another good use of this 'Deltic' ability to recover from checks, was when time had to be regained on an out-of-course diversion. Such was the case on 24 July 1969 following an accident at Sandy which caused all traffic to be diverted via Cambridge to regain the main line at Hitchin. Among several diverted 'Deltics' was D9021 *Argyll and Sutherland Highlander* hauling the 11.00 King's Cross to Newcastle.

A rather strange sighting was made on 2 August when D9008 *The Green Howards* arrived at Scarborough with empty coaching stock and then worked to Filey Holiday Camp. One would have thought that, particularly at that time of the year, D9008's power could have been better utilized elsewhere, but this sort of thing was, in later years, to become more a part of the life of the 'Deltics'.

Ten days later, on 12 August, an incident at King's Cross station showed just how indifferent the 'Deltics' could be at times. D9002 *The King's Own Yorkshire Light Infantry* stood in the platform attached to the stock of the 17.05 departure, but immediately before starting time the driver was unable to release the brakes. A Class '24' was quickly summoned and dragged D9002 off the train into a siding. Meanwhile, D9019 *Royal Highland Fusilier,* which had been rostered for the 18.00 departure, was immediately commandeered and attached to the 17.05 which finally got away at 17.32. Despite a rigorous attempt to win back time, running to Peterborough in 59.5 mins net with a maximum speed of 103 mph, D9019 was detained at Peterborough North Station for 6 mins to let 'The Yorkshire Pullman' overtake on the goods line — a sad reward for such a good effort.

Another failure befell D9016 *Gordon Highlander* at Peterborough North Station whilst hauling the 08.00 from King's Cross to Edinburgh on 15 November. No other air-braked locomotive was available, so Class '31' D5600 was put on as pilot with the intention of going on to Doncaster. By this time the 08.20 had arrived from King's Cross and was held to follow the delayed train out. Then it was decided to remove both D9016 and D5600 in favour of Class '47' D1764, which was quickly summoned from a southbound cement train. Eventually the 08.20 King's Cross-Leeds was allowed away, closely followed by D1764 on the 08.00.

In such times of trouble, the 'Deltics' have had to resort to any assistance, no matter how inadequate, in a crisis. One such incident happened to D9019 *Royal Highland Fusilier* when it failed at Heaton Car-

The Deltic
Years in
Colour

D9012 Crepello *speeds
through Darlington on the
inaugural down 'Elizabethan',
18 June 1962* (D. Carter).

A then un-named D9006 passes York on the up 'Flying Scotsman' in 1964 (D. Carter).

D9010, also still un-named, reverses into Stockton-on-Tees station with a Sunday train diverted down the coast line in 1962. Engineering works in the station necessitated the train going around the back of the station then reversing wrong line into the platform (D. Carter).

*Years of transition —
D9001* St Paddy *passes
stand-by locomotive Gresley
'A3' 60106* Flying Fox *at
York, 11 March 1964* (D.
Carter).

D9011 The Royal
Northumberland
Fusiliers *departs from
Ripon heading the 'Queen of
Scots' Pullman, 11 June
1964. The locomotive,
coaches and route are all now
non-existant* (D. Carter).

D9001 St Paddy *leaves Darlington Bank Top on the inaugural up 'North Eastern' service to King's Cross, 15 June 1964 (D. Carter).*

An unidentified 'Deltic' overflowing with excess water scooped up from Danby Wiske troughs, November 1964 (D. Carter).

Resplendent in the two-tone green livery, and train of maroon stock, D9008 The Green Howards *passes Castle Hills Junction, Northallerton, with a down working, 17 August 1965* (D. Carter).

Left *D9014* The Duke of Wellington's Regiment, *the final 'Deltic' to remain in green livery, but with the addition of the rather ungainly-looking all-over yellow nose-ends, departs from Newcastle for Edinburgh, circa 1968* (D. Carter).

Left *Between 1966 and 1969, the 'Deltics' were repainted in the new rail blue livery.* 9013 The Black Watch, *still with the full number panel, leaves Peterborough on a down working circa 1973-4* (D. Carter).

Right *55002* The King's Own Yorkshire Light Infantry *sporting the new blue livery and the new modifications to the train indicator panels passes Hitchin on 17 April 1975. (Note also the newly installed supports for overhead electrification)* (D. Carter).

Left *During 1976, the 'Deltics' began to appear with their headcode panels completely blanked off all but two headlights.* 55013 The Black Watch *arrives at York on an up Edinburgh to King's Cross working, 21 August 1978* (H. Watson).

Below left *55012* Crepello *speeds north past Bradbury, Co Durham, on 28 September 1979. With the wind in the right direction, a 'Deltic' could be heard for miles at this location!* (D. Carter).

Right *55012* Crepello, *specially turned out by Finsbury Park Depot, arrives at Darlington Bank Top on the down inaugural 'Silver Jubilee', 8 June 1977* (D. Carter).

Below *During 1979, all the Finsbury Park 'Deltics' gained white window surrounds. The much-enhanced* Crepello *takes a well-earned rest at King's Cross, 28 February 1981* (D. Carter).

55015 Tulyar, *also with white cab surrounds, arrives at York on an up Edinburgh to King's Cross extra on 7 April 1980* (H. Watson).

By March 1981, Tulyar *was fitted with 'Rocket 150' commemorative plaques on both ends, and is seen here departing from York on the 15.50 to King's Cross* (D. Carter).

55018 Ballymoss *passes
Ferryhill, Co Durham, on the
up Edinburgh to Plymouth train
in early 1981* (H. Watson).

'Deltics' at rest: 55004
Queen's Own Highlander
waits between 'sleeper' duties at
Edinburgh Haymarket Depot in
the company of 47438, 21 June
1981 (H. Watson).

55008 The Green Howards
at York Depot, 31 October
1981. It still retains its
regimental crest at this date – the
only 'Deltic' to do so
(H. Watson).

A general view of York Depot with 55008 The Green Howards *(one of only two 'Deltics' to retain the 'white spot' indicator panels until withdrawal) in the foreground with 55017* The Durham Light Infantry *in the distance, 31 October 1981* (H. Watson).

*A reminder of former glories:
55002* The King's Own
Yorkshire Light Infantry,
*repainted in the original green
livery by the NRM,
photographed soon after passing
the unique Newport Bridge,
Middlesbrough, whilst heading
a special from Newcastle to
Whitby, 2 August 1981* (D.
Carter).

Above *55002* The King's Own Yorkshire Light Infantry *passes York Depot in grand style heading north on the 'Celtic Deltic' railtour, 31 October 1981* (H. Watson).

Right *Saved for the future: the 'Deltic' Preservation Society's 55019* Royal Highland Fusilier *makes a guest appearance at the 'Scotrail' Haymarket Open Day, 24 August 1985, alongside Class '47/7' 47715 freshly painted and named* Haymarket (H. Watson).

D9014 The Duke of Wellington's Regiment: *the final 'Deltic' to remain in green livery departs from Newcastle for Edinburgh* (D. Carter).

riage Sidings, Newcastle, hauling the empty stock of the 11.00 Newcastle to King's Cross. The only help available was Class '08' D3926, which was coupled to the rear of this 13-coach load and propelled it and the 'Deltic' into Newcastle Central, where the '08' removed D9019 to Gateshead Shed. Class '47' D1969 was quickly acquired and left for London at 11.40.

A sad event, for many, took place at the end of November, when D9014 *The Duke of Wellington's Regiment* was out-shopped from Doncaster Works in the rail-blue livery. D9014 was the last 'Deltic' to retain the splendid two-tone green livery which so much enhanced the appearance of the 'Deltics' in the 'sixties, and so 1969 came to an end with all the 'Deltics' running in the new relatively drab guise — the price of progress!

New Year's Eve provided one last memory of 1969, when the unusual combination of D9003 *Meld* towing the dead Class '47' D1660 *City of Truro* and its train, the 08.50 up Hull service, was noted at Grantham.

1970

'...another year of higher speeds and cuts in journey times...'

By 1970 the East Coast Main Line services had become reasonably punctual, with the timekeeping of certain trains being particularly good. As part of re-alignment work on the main line before the introduction of still faster schedules in May 1970, British Rail Engineering Department filled in a bend of the River Ouse near Offord to enable them to ease the reverse curves following the river which had long been subject to a 70 mph speed restriction, thus allowing faster speeds for all classes of trains over this stretch of line. Another major work completed for the May speed-up was the reduction of the four-track layout through Durham station to two down and one up, so enabling the curve at the viaduct end of the station to be eased, allowing an increase from 30 mph to 50 mph for passing trains. Yet another major project was the new alignment of about 1.5 miles of track at Newton Hall just north of Durham, which eliminated a 55 mph curve and was brought into use on 20 April.

On 6 January, the 09.15 Aberdeen to Glasgow Queen Street rolled into Dundee 47 minutes late behind D9008 *The Green Howards*, a very rare performer indeed on this train and probably appropriated at a moment's notice by Ferryhill Depot to stand in for a failure. It seems strange that during this period the 'Deltics' were used on such occasions as failures to Edinburgh and Aberdeen trains when, on the East Coast Main Line itself, some 'Deltic' turns were being worked by Class '46's and '47's. Such was the case on 3 January, when Class '46' D178 headed the 13.45 Edinburgh to King's Cross and Class '47' D1111 had charge of the 16.00 for London (both normally 'Deltic' turns).

Just as Class '47's were the first choice to help out 'Deltics' in trouble so the reverse was the case; on 1 February D1993 sustained a brake failure at Newark whilst heading an up freightliner train. Nearly 90 minutes passed before the train was propelled into a loop clear of the main line by none other than D9003 *Meld*. Further north, a rare appearance was noted in the early hours of 11 March when an unidentified 'Deltic' was spotted on a freightliner train heading west through the Bellshill area of Glasgow.

The nameplate and crest of 9008 The Green Howards contrasts with the work-stained bodyside, no doubt due to hard running, bad weather and accumulated high mileage between cleaning. (The two small vents on each side of the crest were to help dissipate battery acid odours) (H. Watson).

On one occasion during the spring of 1970, D9015 *Tulyar* arrived 9 minutes early at Wakefield on the 11.30 high-speed 8-coach train from King's Cross to Leeds. The train's time must have been 135 mins for the 175.85 miles to Wakefield, a start-to-stop average of 78.1 mph which must have been a near record at that time. In fact, the first down train of the accelerated Eastern Region timetable on 4 May was the 07.45 from King's Cross to Newcastle, hauled by D9012 *Crepello*. Passengers were given a souvenir card of the timings and those in the dining-car were treated to a glass of champagne. *Crepello* reached Darlington (232 miles) 4.5 mins early at 10.39, and although being held there until the scheduled departure time at 10.45 hrs still reached Newcastle one minute early. Members of the train crew were presented with travelling alarm clocks, and a large cigar went to *Crepello*'s driver as a bonus. Similar festivities attended the arrival at King's Cross of the 07.35 from Newcastle, hauled by D9014, which also reached London one minute early.

By contrast, earlier that spring D9012 had found itself on unfamiliar territory on 27 March when it was used on one of several freight trains diverted from the main line because of engineering work, and travelling via Temple Mills and Cambridge to gain the joint line to Lincoln and Doncaster.

D9012 was in the news again on 17 May when it was chartered to lead an RCTS special to Diss in Norfolk from Leeds, travelling via Chesterfield, Peterborough, March and Ely. After arrival, D9012 ran light to Norwich for servicing whilst its stock rested in a siding at Diss. Meanwhile, another unusual turn for a 'Deltic' was worked by D9000 *Royal Scots Grey* on 7 April when a DMU failed and was replaced by two outer-suburban coaches and D9000 on the 09.24 stopping train from Peterborough to King's Cross. With such super-power, the train left 29 mins late and arrived at King's Cross only 16 mins down.

The crossing gate victim – 9000 Royal Scots Grey. Although taken after preservation, this photo shows 9000 in the same livery it wore at the time of the accident (S. Cholmondeley).

An interesting arrival at Gushetfaulds Freightliner Depot, Glasgow, on 3 June was D9004 *Queen's Own Highlander* with the 16.40 train from Stockton-on-Tees. D9004 had taken charge in the Edinburgh area after the failure of Class '37' 37166. The 'Deltic' returned on the 01.30 Gushetfaulds to Stockton-on-Tees freightliner train, but how far is not known.

Day-to-day running of any class of locomotive must eventually have its casualties, such as the case of D9000 *Royal Scots Grey* which on 20 July, whilst hauling the 08.00 King's Cross to Edinburgh, ran into some crossing gates at speed near Claypole. Fortunately, no serious damage was sustained and the train proceeded some 25 mins later.

The scene at Gateshead Depot in 1970 had not changed from the mid to late 'sixties. 'Deltics' noted on shed on the afternoon of 21 August were D9006 *The Fife and Forfar Yeomanry*, D9007 *Pinza* and D9020 *Nimbus*, interspersed with Classes '25', '37', '40', '46' and '47', and also 'Claytons' D8589/94/95 and 98.

By mid-summer the accelerated timetable had been in force long enough to assess its merits, and observations on a summer Saturday in August at Peterborough proved that the 1970 service, at least on that particular day, was a model of timekeeping. All trains booked for 'Deltic' haulage worked as programmed, with Classes '40', '46' and

'47' on other services. In fact, on 1 September, D9016 *Gordon Highlander* set up a record, if a somewhat undisciplined performance, on the 15.50 King's Cross to Leeds. The train passed Peterborough in 56.5 mins, Doncaster in 111.5 mins and Wakefield in 131 mins, and arrived at Leeds in 147.5 mins from London.

Although *Gordon Highlander*'s run showed what a 'Deltic' with 8 coaches could do, a run recorded by O. S. Nock showed what a 'Deltic' could still achieve with a 11-coach train at a gross weight of 385 tons north of York on the then 10.59 service to Edinburgh. The train was headed by D9010 *The King's Own Scottish Borderer*, and departed from York 6 minutes late; after negotiating the initial sharply-curved section to Skelton, D9010 went ahead in great style, despite the weather of snow and sleet. With the aid of continuous colour-light signalling and efficient windscreen wipers, there was no difficulty in sighting signals, even at high speed. By Tollerton, D9010 was doing 95 mph and averaged 99.5 mph over the next 29.2 miles to Eryholme. Speed was maintained at a remarkably even figure with a maximum of 101 mph and, as D9010 neared Eryholme, the speed was reduced to just under the 80 mph stipulated from that point onwards. Darlington was reached in 32 mins 52 secs from York — a start-to-stop average of 80.7 mph and a gain of just over 4 minutes on the schedule.

Although D9010 spent a minute over time at Darlington, the schedule included some recovery time and Newcastle was reached one minute early. After leaving Newcastle, the snow, which by then was heavy and pitching thickly at Forest Hall and Killingworth, cleared by the time D9010 passed Morpeth. The scheduled time for the 66.9 miles from Newcastle to Berwick was 62 mins, inclusive of 3 mins recovery time, and with strict observance of speed restrictions D9010 had its work cut out to keep time. In fact, with a severe permanent way slack near Lucker, D9010 was 3 mins down on passing Belford, and a further check before Tweedmouth prevented the 3 mins recovery time between Belford and Berwick being used to regain fully the loss. As a result, D9010 called into Berwick just one minute late.

A study of the speeds around 1970 reveals that throughout from Newcastle to Berwick it was the speed restrictions rather than the locomotive capacity that governed locomotive performance on that section. North of Berwick at that time the whole line was subject to a maximum speed of 75 mph with restrictions to 60 mph for some distance through Granthouse, 65 mph at Burnmouth and Ayton and 70 mph at a point between Cockburnspath and Innerwick. The booked time for D9010 on this particular day between Berwick and Edinburgh was 58 mins and included a 4-min recovery margin. The only permanent way check D9010 experienced on this last lap of its journey was a very short one to 60 mph between Innerwick and Dunbar, and so, with a clear road on to Edinburgh, D9010 covered the last 57.5 miles in 54 mins 35 secs, arriving in the Scottish capital 3 mins early.

On 27-28 August, due to a derailment at Granthouse which completely blocked the main line, a number of 'Deltic'-hauled trains, in-

55010 (9010) The King's Own Scottish Borderer, *the 'Deltic' featured in the magnificent run described on page 69, accelerates away from a Darlington stop on a down King's Cross to Edinburgh service (note the bags of mail in the front coach).*

cluding the 19.55 'Aberdonian' from King's Cross and the 22.15 (also from London), were diverted from Newcastle via Carlisle and Carstairs to reach Edinburgh. Later in the year, on 15 November, this same route came in useful again when services were diverted due to engineering works at Dunbar. One 'Deltic' noted taking the diversion was D9019 *Royal Highland Fusilier* on an Aberdeen-King's Cross train.

So 1970 came to a close with the 'Deltics' having completed yet another year of higher speeds and cuts in journey times. Also, it seems that their reliability was high, for on a visit to Doncaster Works on 28 October, not a single 'Deltic' was seen standing out in the yard although, no doubt, there may have been one or two inside.

1971

'...their performance quality had steadily improved with the passage of time...'

The year started with a bang for the 'Deltics'. The new 1971 timetable saw them allocated to the 'Flying Scotsman' service, covering the 393 miles between London and Edinburgh in 5¾ hours. There was also the introduction of an all-sleeper train, the 'Night Capitals', and the revival of the 'Night Scotsman'. There were accelerations of between 4 and 14 mins on some Anglo-Scottish trains as well as other services. Both the 09.00 King's Cross to Newcastle and the 10.25 up from Leeds had journey times cut by 12 mins, and the 13.15 and 15.20 from Newcastle saved 13 and 14 mins respectively on the 269-mile run. The 09.20 from King's Cross to Leeds was re-timed to leave at 09.10 and conveyed a through portion for Hull.

The 'Night Capitals' left Edinburgh at 22.30 and London at 23.10 replacing combined day-coach and sleeping-car trains, and the name 'Night Scotsman' was resumed by the 23.30 from Edinburgh and the 23.35 from London. The 'Aberdonian' was also re-titled the 'Night Aberdonian'.

During the winter and spring of 1970-71, Class '47's substituted for 'Deltics' on several occasions. The reason for this was that the 'Deltics' were being taken into Doncaster Works for the provision of generators to supply current for electric train heating, for which a total of around 300 hp had to be taken from the main generator. D9007 *Pinza* was initially selected and modified so that power for the electric train heating was obtained from one engine only — the trouble was that this engine had to be worked extra hard to obtain the required voltage. Needless to say, this idea was no good in practice, so the next step was to take D9009 *Alycidon* on 17 October 1970 and alter the idea completely; power for the heating was provided by both generators when idling, but when the engine was under load the full power was produced by the power unit leading in the direction of travel. The snag here was what would happen if one engine had failed, whereby no heating would be available. This was solved after further modifications had been carried out; if one engine failed or cut out, the other engine took over and provided cur-

55007 (9007) Pinza, *the first 'Deltic' to feature in the electric current supply trials for electric train heating passes through Darlington on an up Edinburgh to King's Cross train.*

rent. This proved successful, and all 22 locomotives were modified, ending with D9007 *Pinza* on 8 December 1971.

During 1971, some of the 'Deltics' celebrated ten years in service and totally disproved what the sceptics forecast back in 1961 — thoughts such as what would happen when BR took over the maintenance from English Electric after five years, and would BR be able to cope with the maintenance to a sufficiently high standard to keep these expensive, sophisticated machines in constant use to meet the demands of the schedules.

Well, there certainly were teething troubles, but nothing that required any radical changes in design, and certainly no decline in availability followed the take-over by BR. Of course, there were temporary breakdowns with the 'Deltics' but, on the whole, no greater than with any other class of diesel. In fact, the record of the 22 'Deltics' was commendably trouble-free. However, the most remarkable feature of the performance of these locomotives was the way in which their performance quality had steadily improved with the passage of time, rather than declined, so that all the sceptics were forced to eat their words.

The year also saw an external change, when the numbers of all 22 locomotives dropped the 'D' prefix, the whole class becoming 9000 to 9021.

So, ten years old, the 'Deltics' were still performing magnificent feats, such as the following run recorded by one of Cecil J. Allen's correspondents. The train was the 15.55 King's Cross to Leeds and Harrogate with 9011 *The Royal Northumberland Fusiliers* hauling a 295-ton gross 8-coach train. The driver's encouragement to speed was a late start of 7 mins — here and there some slight liberties were taken with speed restrictions, but nothing serious. By Hatfield, with speed having risen from 80 to 86 mph up the 1 in 200 from Wood Green to Potters Bar, the first 1.75 mins had been recovered, and by Langley the speed had reached 100 mph, but then a signal check to 70 mph caused a loss of $\frac{1}{2}$ min. Before Three Counties, however, the three-figure rate had been re-attained and now, for about 33 miles on end, 9011 ran entirely between 100 and 106 mph with a time of 15 mins 45 secs from Hitchin to Huntingdon, and 100 mph still maintained to the top of the 1 in 200 from Huntingdon to milepost 62.

At the beginning of Stilton Fen, speed was reduced to the pre-scribed 80 mph, but had risen to 89 mph by Yaxley. Peterborough was passed in the then incredibly fast time of 52 mins 31 secs, with 9011 now only 1.5 mins late. The time of 19 mins 29 secs for the 29.1 miles from Peterborough to Grantham, including the entire climb to Stoke, was also magnificent. On the easier stretch between Essendine and Little Bytham, 106 mph was reached, followed by a minimum of 100 mph up the 1 in 200 to milepost $95\frac{1}{2}$ and 95 mph maintained up the final 1 in 178 to Stoke Summit. From King's Cross, the 100.1 miles to Stoke had taken 68 mins 30 secs and Grantham, a further 15.45 miles, was passed in 12 mins, 9011 now running 2 mins early.

The customary 100 mph or slightly over was maintained from Barkston South to Claypole, and after the 80 mph Newark slack 9011 accelerated to 99 mph on the level, before the long and severe permanent way check then in force beyond Crow Park, which cost about 3 mins running time. After the Retford slack there was a brief 102 mph at Ran-skill and an unusual 100 mph between Bawtry and Rossington 80 mph service slacks; a subsequent signal check probably cost about 45 secs.

So, 9011 was through Doncaster, 155.95 miles from King's Cross, in 110 mins 12 secs, or about 106 mins net – 45 secs early. There was lit-tle scope for speed onwards to Leeds and 9011 at no point exceeded 75 mph here, nor indeed needed to; the pitfall slowing at Fitzwilliam cost 1 min and Wakefield was passed on time. The timing of 13 minutes for the 6 miles from Ardsley to Leeds, including 2 mins recovery, was un-necessarily generous and was easily cut to 9 mins 32 secs so that 9011 rolled triumphantly into Leeds City Station 145 mins 40 secs after leav-ing King's Cross, or 140 mins net (3.25 mins early), and in 16 minutes net less than the 156 mins scheduled. One could hardly have a finer ex-ample of 'Deltic' ability than this.

Quite a different task fell to 9021 *Argyll and Sutherland Highlander* on 21 January. The royal train conveying the Queen from Kings Lynn to Stirling on the previous day was stabled overnight at Larbert. On the 21st, it went forward to Stirling hauled by 9021, whose name happened to be the regiment which the Queen was to visit and whose museum is housed in Stirling Castle.

After the astounding 'Deltic' performance and availability des-cribed in the last few pages, the tables must now be turned, for during April and May the 'Deltics' suffered a spate of failures for various reasons. On 1 April, the 07.25 Leeds to King's Cross arrived in the capital behind Class '47' No 1760, and the same day the 15.55 King's

In connection with Royal train operation, two 'Deltics' (9010 and 9019) were fitted with a removable circular plate on their nose ends for the insertion of a radio communication system between driver and train. The plate is visible above the right-hand buffer of 9019 Royal Highland Fusilier *(S. Cholmondeley).*

Cross to Leeds had to be powered by Class '45' No 53 *Royal Tank Regiment*. On 10 April, 9010 *The King's Own Scottish Borderer* was removed from the 08.00 King's Cross to Edinburgh at Doncaster. South of Edinburgh the failure rate, from which the whole East Coast Main Line suffered, caused the up 'Flying Scotsman' to be headed by Class '47' No 1996 on 8 May. On 15 May, the 12.00 Edinburgh-King's Cross found itself behind Class '40' No 264, and was thus 40 per cent under power. However, 9012 *Crepello* did manage to reach Newcastle before failing on the 08.00 King's Cross to Edinburgh on 18 May, which was then taken on to Edinburgh by Class '47' No 1503. On 21 May, 9013 *The Black Watch* failed at Huntingdon whilst hauling the 'Yorkshire Pullman' and was piloted forward by Class '31' No 5610. Earlier the same day, 5610 had given assistance to Class '40' No 245 from Marshmoor to Peterborough when it failed on the down 'Highwayman'. Thankfully, this period soon passed and the 'Deltics' got back into their stride once more.

The introduction to revenue-earning duty of the first Mk IID coaches on the East Coast Main Line, with which the 'Deltics' were to become very accustomed, took place on 12 July. The stock immediately became quite popular with passengers, with its air conditioning and good riding qualities. Alas, whilst hauling this type of stock three days later, 9002 *The King's Own Yorkshire Light Infantry* was in trouble at Hitchin with the 14.00 King's Cross to Edinburgh after one of its engines had failed. Although after many attempts the driver managed to start the engine, a standby locomotive was requested to take over at Peterborough.

The summer of 1971 brought with it a fair share of unusual 'Deltic' workings, such as during May when 9010 *The King's Own Scottish Borderer* was used on several freight workings. On 13 May, 9010 headed an air-braked carflat train from Finsbury Park to Doncaster, the train originating from Ramsgate. The next day, 9010 was again noted on the 20.30 Hull to Temple Mills freight. Another unusual duty was the use of 9006 *The Fife and Forfar Yeomanry* on Saturday 26 June to head the Saturdays-only 08.40 Paignton to Newcastle train on the last leg of its journey from York onwards to Newcastle.

Amongst other unusual duties during that summer was the use of 9004 *Queen's Own Highlander* to head the 14.10 King's Cross to Newcastle parcels; for economy reasons, the locomotive was using only one engine. Later in the summer, on 4 September, 9005 *The Prince of Wales's Own Regiment of Yorkshire* was seen heading a parcels train past Low Fell near Gateshead. On 9 September, 9013 *The Black Watch* provided super-power for the 07.20 Lincoln to King's Cross, whilst later that month Lincoln also witnessed the sight of 9010 *The King's Own Scottish Borderer* running on trial from Doncaster to Lincoln and returning light engine. But perhaps the most unusual use of a 'Deltic' during the year came on 16 November when 9000 *Royal Scots Grey* arrived at Derby on a late evening mail and parcels train from Peterborough to Crewe. This was the first appearance of a 'Deltic' at Derby, and 9000 returned to Peterborough the next morning on a parcels train from Bristol.

The year came to a close at what was the beginning of a transitional period for the 'Deltics', during which they would begin to show their worth on occasional freight and parcels trains, while at the same time spread further their wide route availability.

1972

'...speeds of up to 100 mph over roughly 80 per cent of the route from King's Cross to Newcastle...'

During the early part of 1972 I visited Gateshead Depot on two occasions (16 January and 2 April) and on both occasions, unusually, no 'Deltics' were to be seen. Also, on 16 April, a Sunday, only 9017 *The Durham Light Infantry* was on shed, whilst 30 April proved little better with only 9014 *The Duke of Wellington's Regiment* and 9015 *Tulyar* on view. Better was 14 May when 9002/11/15 and 21 were all on shed, along with a stranger — Class '31' No 5527.

The early part of 1972 saw the beginning of improvements to the East Coast Main Line costing £2.5 million. These improvements were expected to be finished in time for the new timetable of May 1973, when a 'Deltic'-hauled express was expected to maintain speeds of up to 100 mph over roughly 80 per cent of the route from King's Cross to Newcastle, reducing the journey to 3 hrs 25 mins for the 269 miles — an average speed of 80 mph. Work in progress included the strengthening and re-aligning of 19 miles of track between Wood Green and Hitchin; re-alignment at Saltersford between High Dyke and Grantham; and re-

A typical 1970s view of Gateshead Depot. Nearest the camera is 46039 (176), followed by 47428 (1536) and 55005 (9005) (H. Watson).

alignment to raise speed restrictions through Selby Station, including the re-modelling of the junction with the Hull line at Barlby North and adjustments of curves. Re-alignment and minor bridge works also took place over the 36 miles between Darlington and Newcastle. At Peterborough the layout was completely re-modelled to provide fast through lines completely independent of the station platforms, and the speed limit of non-stop trains was raised dramatically from 20 to 100 mph.

Before the start of these modifications, and whilst they were progressing, the 'Deltics' made some very fine runs but despite a great deal of fast running at or around 100 mph, the overall speeds tended to lag behind those then being regularly attained on certain other routes both in Great Britain and in Europe. The old Peterborough layout, with its 20 mph restriction, accounted for about 4.5 mins, whilst if one was able to run at full speed from Skelton box, north of York, to Escrick, the 8.8 miles could be covered in only 6 mins or less. However, with a little pruning elsewhere, the prospects of a regular 80 mph service between London and Newcastle were reasonably bright, and at a time of 3 hrs 20 mins made the railway strongly competitive with the internal airlines.

It was around this period that O. S. Nock received details from an acquaintance of a journey from Newcastle to King's Cross on the 'Flying Scotsman', loaded to 12 coaches grossing 430 tons full, and headed by 9020 *Nimbus*. Quite apart from locomotive performance, the run was of particular interest in demonstrating the effect of the then recent improvements to the line at various locations. There was Durham, for example, passed at 51 mph and the Aycliffe curve taken at 80 mph, enabling the apparently sharp allowance of 35 mins from Newcastle to Darlington to be cut by 1.25 mins, despite a signal check. It was also apparently easy to gain 1.5 mins on the point-to-point time of 19 mins for the 28.3 miles from Northallerton to Skelton box, turning a booked average of 89.4 mph into an actual 96.7 mph. However, because of a signal check before Darlington and a more severe one at Cowton, *Nimbus* was 1.25 mins late through York. The allowance of only 9 mins for the 14.1 miles from Darlington to Northallerton seemed then unduly tight, and the Cowton check had cost *Nimbus* about 2.75 mins.

South of York there were many checks in addition to the regular speed restrictions. The viaduct repairs at Bawtry were not then completed and there were permanent way slacks, albeit of less severity, at Moss and Grantham. But the most unusual check for this route was an interruption of the 100 mph flight from Stoke Tunnel down to Peterborough with signal checks at both Essendine and Tallington. Although *Nimbus* recovered to 82 mph by Werrington Junction, all and more of the 3 mins recovery allowance between Essendine and Werrington Junction had been swallowed up and the train passed through Peterborough 1.5 mins late. The various checks up to this point had, however, accounted for no less than 12.5 mins between them — $\frac{1}{2}$ min for Darlington North, 2.75 mins for Cowton, 1.75 mins for Moss, 3 mins for Bawtry Viaduct, 1 min for Grantham and 3.5 mins for Essendine and Tallington. The net time from Newcastle to passing Peter-

This photograph shows to good effect the rather graceful yet bulbous proportions of a 'Deltic', emphasized by the all-over blue livery as opposed to the two-tone green. A very clean 9019 Royal Highland Fusilier *stands adjacent to Darlington Bank Top Station* (S. Cholmondeley).

borough was, thus, no more than 150 mins, an average speed of 76.8 mph from the start.

From Peterborough, *Nimbus* got a clear road until after Finsbury Park and made full use of it. Holding the speed first to the raised limit of 80 mph across the Fens and then attaining 88 mph beyond, *Nimbus* went on to clear Abbots Ripton bank at a minimum of 86 mph. Then the speed lay entirely at between 99 and 105 mph without a break from Huntingdon to Three Counties, an average speed of 101 mph. The result of this spell of finely sustained high speed, with the aid of 3 mins recovery time from Sandy, was that *Nimbus* passed Hitchin 7 minutes early! This gain was increased to 8 mins by Potters Bar, but after this *Nimbus* was eased back just a little. After this outstanding performance, it was inevitable that delays would be experienced in the final approach to King's Cross and *Nimbus* was, in fact, stopped for 3 mins at Belle Isle. The net time to Finsbury Park was 203.25 mins, representing an average of 78.5 mph from the start, proving yet again the capability of these fine machines.

Besides completing such arduous tasks as the aforementioned run,

the 'Deltics' seemed, by 1972, to be used more and more often on mundane duties, such as on 9 January when 9018 *Ballymoss* was used on the 08.45 Peterborough-Hitchin, and then the 10.12 Hitchin-King's Cross. Another 'Deltic' was found on unusual ground on 14 February, when 9005 *The Prince of Wales's Own Regiment of Yorkshire* was utilized on the 14.04 King's Cross to Cambridge, returning on the 16.30 from Cambridge in place of the rostered DMU. Meanwhile, on 1 March, 9006 *The Fife and Forfar Yeomanry* ventured further north when it was seen travelling west through Falkirk. It was during the next month, on 14 April, that 9006 worked probably one of the most unusual workings to fall to a 'Deltic', being noted on the 00.05 Peterborough to Castle Bromwich, Birmingham, cement train — exactly how far it ventured I do not know. To return to London, a stranger at Stratford Depot on 25 March was 9007 *Pinza*, in the company of 'Hymek' No 7001.

Many things contributed to a 'Deltic' being found off its beaten track. One such incident happened on 23 May when, due to a railmen's work to rule, 9011 *The Royal Northumberland Fusiliers* became a unique visitor to Sheffield Midland Station. No 9011 was heading a Newcastle-

King's Cross train when it was diverted from York via Rotherham to Sheffield, where its train was terminated. The passengers continued their journey to London's St Pancras via the Midland line services.

Five days later, on 28 May, 9003 *Meld* found itself involved in an accident, although luckily it received no serious damage. The train involved was the 11.00 Edinburgh-King's Cross, composed of air-conditioned Mk IID stock, which became derailed at Chathill in Northumberland. Although running for some 300 yds off the track, the derailed coaches remained upright and only two people required hospital treatment. Passengers were picked up by a down train headed by Class '40' No 239 and returned north.

A remarkable run was made on the night of 16-17 June when the 23.55 King's Cross to Newcastle suffered the failure of 9007 *Pinza* at departure time. The train was instantly propelled up the bank to Finsbury Park by a Class '31', where Class '47' No 1936 was substituted and, although leaving 63 minutes late, was only 9 minutes late on arrival at Newcastle. Sparks must really have flown that night, and it just goes to show what magnificent substitutes the Class '47's were.

During the year, the 'Deltics' proved to be a popular choice at depot open days and station exhibitions. One such occasion at Newcastle Central Station on 18 June featured 9017 *The Durham Light Infantry* alongside Class '47' No 1577, Class '31' No 5856 and one steam locomotive, 'A4' No 4498 *Sir Nigel Gresley*, along with many items of rolling stock. Later in the year, on 10 September, *Sir Nigel Gresley* was again on show in the company of 'Deltic' 9010 *The King's Own Scottish Borderer* at Thornaby Depot Open Day. Among the other special guests was Class '47' No 1576, in impeccable condition and giving footplate rides, along with the 'A4', up and down the yard, while other steam engines on view included Moors Line 'K1' No 2005 and 'J27' No 65894. BR stock included a brand new Mk IID coach, while also on view around the depot was its allocation of Class '03's, '08's, '31's, '37's and '47's, interspersed with visitors from distant depots.

Other 'Deltics' attending open days were 9005 *The Prince of Wales's Own Regiment of Yorkshire* at Staveley, Barrow Hill Depot, on 3 September and 9021 *Argyll and Sutherland Highlander*, which featured at Scotland's 'Railfair 72' Exhibition held at Eastfield Depot, Glasgow, on 16-17 September.

During July, the engineering works involved in the upgrading of the whole East Coast Main Line had reached Scotland. The intensity of these works at Dunbar on Sunday 23 July caused all trains to be diverted via Carlisle, Beattock and Carstairs to reach Edinburgh and vice versa. Two 'Deltics' noted at Carlisle were 9006 and 9017, and no doubt there were many more.

On 12 August, the 09.40 Edinburgh-Plymouth train arrived at Newcastle hauled by 9017 *The Durham Light Infantry*. In fact, in 1979, even after the advent of the HST working, this duty would be regularly 'Deltic'-hauled as far as York and returning to Edinburgh from York on the return working.

Always a good stand-in for a failed 'Deltic' — one of the popular Class '46's, 46035 (172), passes through Co Durham on a heavy train of coiled steel (S. Cholmondeley).

The early part of September witnessed another spate of 'Deltic' failures. On the 12th, 9018 *Ballymoss* suffered a partial loss of power soon after departure with the 18.00 King's Cross to Newcastle and was removed at New Barnet; after some delay the train continued headed by Class '31' No 5606. Another unscheduled stop of 11 mins was made at Doncaster when 9016 *Gordon Highlander* took over from 5606, arriving at Newcastle 89 mins late. Later in the month, on the 16th, 9018 failed again, this time at York with King's Cross to Edinburgh express, and was assisted north by Class '45' No 112.

During November, the 16.28 Doncaster to King's Cross saw a variety of power, the smallest of which was Class '31' No 5619 on 11 November. However, the train had super-power on three other occasions: on 16 November it was double-headed by 9015 *Tulyar* and Class '47' No 1580; on 27 November by 9012 *Crepello* and No 1778; and on 20 November by 9004 *Queen's Own Highlander* and Class '46' No 164.

A further unusual 'Deltic' working around this time was the use of 9017 *The Durham Light Infantry* on the 21.30 King's Cross to Hertford North as a replacement for a Class '31'.

The year came to a close with the 'Deltics' making still faster times as the improvements to the East Coast Main Line progressed; they had also stolen the limelight throughout the year at various open days and exhibitions.

1973

'What for many people signalled the beginning of the end came during May and June...'

A milestone in the exclusive life of the 'Deltic' came during mid-January, when 9010 *The King's Own Scottish Borderer* became the first member of the class to reach 2,000,000 miles since its introduction in 1961 and was, in fact, the first diesel-electric locomotive in the world to reach such a mileage in less than 12 years. Nos 9000 and 9006 were destined to be the next to reach this figure and all three, by coincidence, were Haymarket, Edinburgh, locomotives.

Although the 'Deltic' fleet had amassed such a high mileage in such a short space of time, due only to their high availability and high standard of maintenance, the class still had 'off days'. One such opened the year; on 2 January, the 14.15 Newcastle to King's Cross suffered an

Safely past the 2,000,000 mile mark, 55010 (9010) The King's Own Scottish Borderer *continues notching up the miles as she powers north out of Darlington past Parkgate Junction.*

engine failure at Darlington, and 9019 *Royal Highland Fusilier* was re-placed by Class '37' No 6702. Although the precise nature of the failure is not known, the front four coaches were covered in oil, which could indicate a burst fuel tank. At York, Class '47' No 1509 took over and reached King's Cross 73 minutes late.

In contrast, let us now turn to an outstanding run by 9006 *The Fife and Forfar Yeomanry*, as recorded by one of O. S. Nock's correspondents. This particular run is all the more interesting in that it features a journey when, due to a blockage at Dunbar, 9006 was diverted from Edinburgh to Newcastle via Carstairs, Carlisle and Hexham. The train concerned was the 12 noon Edinburgh to King's Cross, weighing some 430 tons full. After getting away from Edinburgh and making a spirited run, 9006 was subject to much delay at Strawfrank Junction, passing there almost 15 mins late on this special re-timed schedule. No times could be gained on the very sharp allowance of only 20 mins from Strawfrank Junction up to Beattock Summit, with a moderate permanent way check at Symington, but from Beattock Station to Kirkpatrick the running was the fastest I have ever heard of over this stretch with a diesel-electric, averaging 97 mph with a maximum of 103 mph near Dinwoodie. Thus, Carlisle was reached only 1.5 mins late, after some severe delays. 9006 was a credit to Haymarket on that day, for once back on her own ground she made a truly magnificent run from Darlington to York.

After a normal start from Darlington, 9006 was doing 80 mph by Eryholme and the 28.2 miles from Danby Wiske to Beningborough took only 16 mins 27 secs, an average of 102.7 mph. 9006 had thus taken only 31 mins 38 secs from Darlington to York with 430 tons of train, featuring an average speed from Otterington to Beningborough (a distance of

The powerful imposing front end of 9019 Royal Highland Fusilier *showing the final position of warning air horns, early-1970s number (9019) complete with data panel, and, below that, the HA Edinburgh Haymarket shed allocation sticker* (S. Cholmondeley).

21 miles) of 104.3 mph. Just how much longer 9006 kept up this performance is not known, as Mr Nock's correspondent left the train at York.

As well as surprise speeds, the 'Deltics' also made surprise appearances. One such occasion laid on for Scottish 'Deltic' fans was the use of 9001 *St Paddy* on 15 February on the 08.05 Edinburgh to Aberdeen and the 12.30 return. Another surprise further south on 29 March was when Gateshead Depot turned out 9016 *Gordon Highlander* to work the 07.00 Newcastle to Edinburgh train — super-power to say the least! Finally, the Glasgow Works Eastfield Open Day on 12 May was enlivened by the sight of an immaculately turned out 9010 *The King's Own Scottish Borderer*, exhibited alongside Class '84' No 84 005 amongst other classes of locomotives.

What for many people signalled the beginning of the end came during May and June 1973, when the prototype HST began to undergo trials on the East Coast Main Line, foreshadowing the demise of the 'Deltics' from top-link work. Even so, and still not to be outdone, the 'Deltics' began regularly working straight through to Harrogate on the 'Yorkshire Pullman' service from London at the beginning of the year. Then, on 9 July, just for a change, 9009 *Alycidon* was commandeered at Leeds to work forward to Bradford with 'The Cornishman', later returning to Leeds with the empty stock.

From Monday 2 July, three Eastern Region trains for businessmen, linking the North-east of England and the West Riding with London, received names. On that day each was 'Deltic'-hauled and given a civic 'send off' from King's Cross. The 'Newcastle Executive' ran from Newcastle at 07.25, calling at Durham and Darlington, and returned from King's Cross at 18.00; the 'Leeds Executive' left Leeds at 07.30, returning at 15.55; and the 'Bradford Executive' ran at 07.20, calling at Wakefield Westgate and returning from London at 16.05.

Other services on the East Coast Main Line were also given a face-lift during 1973 in terms of shorter journey times. One such, the 'Tees-Tyne Pullman', was re-timed to reach York in 150 mins from King's Cross, and to show how the 'Deltics' coped is a log of the journey on the second day of the new timetable, once again recorded by O. S. Nock.

Despite checks in the early stages which had caused a loss of 3 mins to Hitchin from King's Cross, Retford (138.6 miles) was passed in 101 mins 18 secs, nearly 6 minutes early and having averaged 93.7 mph over the previous 106.7 miles from Hitchin. Various checks followed, but York was reached in 147 mins 6 secs, a net time of 139 mins. This run was remarkable in that, having regained the 3 mins of initial arrears by Huntingdon, the 'Deltic' was not unduly extended onwards to Grantham, and the average speed over the 36.6 miles from Abbots Ripton to Stoke box was no more than 94.5 mph, passing Peterborough itself at 92 mph.

On the up road, another of Mr Nock's logs gives details of a good run on the 17.00 from Newcastle with one of the limited-load 8-coach trains, timed to cover the 203.7 miles from Darlington to Stevenage in 146 mins, an average of 83.8 mph start-to-stop. The train, hauled by

9006 *The Fife and Forfar Yeomanry* left Darlington 3.75 mins late. On this run, the consistency with which the maximum speeds touched 105 mph suggests that this might be a case of 9006's speedometer reading slightly low. Apart from the individual maxima, one can note the averages of 102.5 mph from Northallerton to Skelton Junction; 101.8 mph from Essendine to Peterborough; and 101 mph from Abbots Ripton to St Neots. The net time must have been around 134.75 mins at an average speed of 90.7 mph — a truly fine performance!

Amongst other services to benefit from the general accelerations of the 1973 timetable were the Hull trains and, thereafter, the frequency with which 'Deltics' were used on the Doncaster to Hull line increased. One of the early appearances was by 9016 *Gordon Highlander* which was noted leaving Goole on the up 'Hull Pullman' on 22 June. As during the previously described run with 9006, Peterborough was passed at 92 mph. This was now possible, for during May, right on schedule, the old 'dog-leg' turn out at the north end of Peterborough North Station was abolished and the new high-speed through lines were opened to allow passing train speeds to be accelerated from 20 to 100 mph.

Another slight external change took place on the 'Deltics', along with every other class of locomotive on BR fitted with headcode panels, during 1973. During March, 9009 *Alycidon* was outshopped from Doncaster Works displaying two prominent white spots on a black background in its headcode panel. This superseded the old four-character headcode numbering which was abandoned. During the latter part of the year BR also introduced a new numbering system, which incorporated in the number the new classification for the 'Deltics' by prefixing the number with 55. From then on, the 'Deltics' became Class '55' and were re-numbered, 9001-9021 becoming 55001-55021 (9000 became 55022). However, it was well into 1974 before all the 'Deltics' acquired their new numbers.

The first 'Deltic' to be fitted with the white-spot-on-black-background indicator panels during the seventies, 55009 (9009) Alycidon, is seen here entering Darlington Bank Top on an up train for London, passing (left) 08268 (3338) and (right) 08004 (3008) (H. Watson).

Not the best deputy for a 'Deltic' failure, but very reliable, the cumbersome Class '40's did well in a crisis. No 40104 leaves Darlington Bank Top on a typical '40' working, the Heaton to Manchester Red Bank parcels (S. Cholmondeley).

One particular 'Deltic' in the news on 10 June was 9004 *Queen's Own Highlander* when, after being on exhibition at Inverness Station with 'A4' *Union of South Africa*, it piloted a Class '24' and '26' as far as Perth on the up 'Royal Highlander'.

Failures noted during the middle to latter half of the year were few. On 31 July, 9004 *Queen's Own Highlander* failed at Newcastle on the 08.00 King's Cross-Edinburgh train with engine trouble, and 9008 *The Green Howards* took the train on to Edinburgh after a slight delay. On 3 September, the 'Aberdonian' suffered a failure at Peterborough with 9013 *The Black Watch* in charge. Class '47' No 1736 towed 9013 and train on to Doncaster, where both locomotives were removed in favour of 9019 *Royal Highland Fusilier*, which continued north more than 100 mins late. Two days later, on the 5th, 9001 *St Paddy* also failed at Peterborough with the 14.00 King's Cross to Edinburgh train. Class '40', re-numbered 40164, was quickly attached to continue north piloting 9001 as far as Doncaster, where *St Paddy* was hastily removed and taken into the Works. Perhaps the most unusual of failures happened to 9013 *The Black Watch* shortly before midnight on 2 December. As 9013 moved

down from Doncaster Depot towards the station, a fire broke out on the locomotive and the local fire brigade had to be quickly summoned. The extent of the fire damage is not known, but 9013 was removed to the Works.

The most unusual appearance of 'Deltics' on the 07.00 Newcastle-Edinburgh occurred frequently towards the end of the year. To use a 'Deltic' on this lightly-loaded train was, indeed, an over-abundance of power! (One unit noted on this service was 9020 *Nimbus* on 16 November.) Another line which was beginning to see more 'Deltics' by late 1973 was that between Edinburgh and Aberdeen, although still not on a regular basis. On 7 December, 55022 *Royal Scots Grey* was noted leaving Aberdeen on the 09.00 to King's Cross.

The year ended with the 'Deltics' still maintaining their position as the front-line power on the East Coast Main Line, but now with an in-filtrator in the shape of the prototype HST showing its capabilities to both enthusiast and public alike.

1974

'Haymarket's 'Deltics' always seemed to be impeccably turned out...'

55005 The Prince of Wales's Own Regiment of Yorkshire *departs from Darlington Bank Top past the DMU Depot on a down express for the north.*

January saw once again the utilization of a 'Deltic' on the London to Cleethorpes service, only this time and thereafter the 'Deltics' were to become used to a more regular pattern on this route. This particular instance was on the 21st, when 55002 *The King's Own Yorkshire Light Infantry* hauled the 08.15 King's Cross to Cleethorpes train, and was also used again on this duty the following day. It was at the time believed to have been the first sighting of a 'Deltic' in the Grimsby area since some main line diversions at the end of 1972. No 55002 returned to London on both days with the 14.15 to King's Cross.

On 22 January, further north in Scotland, 55005 *The Prince of Wales's Own Regiment of Yorkshire* was a notable sight heading towards Dundee, running light in the company of Class '40' 40165. The reason for this working was not known, but was probably that 55005 had

worked north to take up an unbalanced working for the south later that day.

During 1974, the Cambridge expresses began to see a wide selection of motive power, ranging from the usual Class '31' or sometimes '47' to 'Deltic' 55003 *Meld* on the 11.30 from King's Cross on 18 February. The reason for such gross misuse of super-power on these services was not disclosed by BR; if shortage of motive power was the reason, why not use Class '40's or '46's as stand-ins, such as was done the next day when 40052 arrived at Cambridge on the 11.30 from King's Cross? Since, by and large the 'Deltic' appearances on Cambridge line trains were a rarity, they must only have been resorted to at times of great stress.

No 55009 *Alycidon* spread her wings a little on 9 March when she travelled as far as Stockport during the early hours on the 21.50 York to Aberystwyth mail train. *Alycidon* returned to York later on the balancing working. This was the first time a 'Deltic' was used on this service but, after the advent of HST working on the East Coast Main Line, 'Deltics' were to become not infrequent power on this train.

York always was a good place for recording and photographing the 'Deltics', and 13 April 1974 was to prove no exception when, in the space of about only two hours, five 'Deltics' (55007/12/15/17 and 21) were noted. At about the same time I visited Doncaster, which was quite different, with the continuous procession of coal trains interspersed with frequent expresses, and a visit to the shed and works. That particular day I logged nine 'Deltics' (55013/17/12/7/4/3/10/1 and 16, in that order). What a sight it was to stand on Doncaster Station and watch a 'Deltic' on a northbound or southbound flyer hurtling past on one of the through lines, almost forcing a path through the continuous flow of freight traffic, and roar away into the distance! On 6 June I paid one of my frequent visits to Ferryhill, Co Durham, and had another good day, noting 55007/17/16/21/14 and 2, in that order. All were in first-class external condition, and sounded the same internally. It is sad now to reflect on days like that, when the 'Deltic' was still an everyday sight.

On 1 June, BR celebrated the centenary of Pullman services in Britain, the very first of which ran from Bradford to St Pancras via the old Midland route. In 1974, the 'Yorkshire Pullman' was the only surviving Pullman running on something near to the original route (Bradford to King's Cross), so the 'Yorkshire Pullman' on Centenary Day was headed by 'Deltic' 55009 *Alycidon*.

Alycidon was back in the news again on 28 August, when it went to the rescue of Class '47' 47418, which had failed between Heaton Carriage Sidings and Newcastle Central Station whilst working empty coaching stock for a southbound departure. Eventually 55009 departed from Central 55 mins late, making a strong, rapid exit once clear of King Edward Bridge Junction, obviously intent on regaining lost time.

The month of September saw 'Deltics' present at two depot open days. The first was at Immingham on the 1st, when 55003 *Meld* featured alongside 47172 and Class '76' electric 76054. The second open day was held at Staveley, Barrow Hill Depot, on the 22nd. By coincidence, this exhibition also again featured Class '76' electric 76054, but this time alongside 'Deltic' 55015 *Tulyar* and the preserved steam locomotive 4472 *Flying Scotsman*.

During the early part of the month, Aberdeen played host to two 'Deltics'. On the 6th, 55019 *Royal Highland Fusilier* worked the 08.55 to King's Cross, while two days later 55013 *The Black Watch* departed on the 10.45 to London. On both occasions the 'Deltics' had worked to Aberdeen on the previous evening's 22.15 sleeper from London.

It was on 26 September that 47418 returned the compliment shown the previous month by 55009, when *Alycidon* rescued it during August when it failed at Newcastle. The favour was returned again when 47418 took over at York from 55002 *The King's Own Yorkshire Light Infantry*, which had developed an oil leak near Peterborough but had managed to reach York before being taken off. The train concerned was the down 'Tees-Tyne Pullman', which eventually left York behind 47418 1 hr 15 mins late.

6 October 1974 is a date that easily sticks in my memory, for it was the day after my marriage to Linda, who has patiently tolerated my enthusiasm for both model and actual railways in all sorts of circumstances throughout Britain and Europe. On that particular day we were on our honeymoon heading north up the A1 trunk road past Granthouse when, over to our left, I couldn't help noticing 55005 *The Prince of Wales's Own Regiment of Yorkshire* in pristine condition heading south, passing Class '26' 26021 on an engineer's train just to the south of the now non-existent Penmanshiel Tunnel. Later that week, on the 10th, I had the chance to sample the sounds of 55019 *Royal Highland Fusilier* departing from Edinburgh Waverley Station — and what a sight it was to see this machine roar out towards Carlton Tunnel and the south! Haymarket's 'Deltics' always seemed to be impeccably turned out, as if someone took a personal pride in each unit, just as Finsbury Park did — but oh, where did Gateshead go wrong? Gateshead's allocation, nine times out of ten, always appeared grubby, but inwardly, thank goodness, lacked nothing and their performance shone as brightly as their northern and southern compatriots.

Another surprise came my way on 6 November at Darlington, when 55003 *Meld* arrived and left for the north, quickly followed by 'Peak' 45039 *The Manchester Regiment*, both of which reside together in model form on my model railway. (No 45039 seemed to follow me everywhere; in 1979 when I was visiting Laira Depot, Plymouth, it passed by, only to be seen later the same day heading over the Saltash Bridge towards Penzance.) It wasn't long before 55008 *The Green Howards* appeared hurtling past on the through lines heading the up 'Flying Scotsman' for King's Cross.

During December it was reported that a 'Deltic' had a regular Sunday working to Keighley on an early morning paper train from Leeds, the locomotive afterwards returning light engine to Holbeck Depot, Leeds. How long this duty lasted I do not know, but it was obviously a

'Deltics' meet on Durham viaduct – 55003 Meld *(left) heads an up King's Cross service out of Durham Station and passes Gateshead-based counterpart 55017* The Durham Light Infantry *hauling a down train for Newcastle.*

fill-in turn for the 'Deltics' concerned during a weekend lay-over period in the Leeds area between more exacting duties.

By the end of the year 'Deltics' 55004/9/10/15/16 and 21 were all running with the two white spots on a black background type of indicator panel, which the whole class were soon to sport.

1975

'...the 'Deltics' were still capable of some fantastic speeds, with apparently little effort.'

The feeling of power is emphasized by this telephoto shot of 55006 The Fife and Forfar Yeomanry *leaving Darlington Bank Top on an up Edinburgh to King's Cross train.*

The year began with the 'Deltics' still predominantly at the top of their profession heading East Coast Main Line crack expresses, together with the Class '47's. One day during January, the 12.30 Leeds to King's Cross, composed of nine coaches, was headed by 55009 *Alycidon* and piloted by Class '46' 46043. With this combination, an 8 mins late start from Wakefield was converted into a 2 mins early arrival at King's Cross.

No 55006 *The Fife and Forfar Yeomanry* was seen on a mundane duty on 8 January when it arrived at Valley Yard, Bradford, on part of a

parcels train diagram from Leeds to Bradford Forster Square. No 55006 returned to Leeds Holbeck Depot light engine, the rest of the turn being worked by the usual Class '31'. The same month also saw the unprecedented sight of two 'Deltics' on the Western Region — 55007 *Pinza* on the 12th and 55001 *St Paddy* on the 19th. Both were sent by Eastern Region for dipped rail joint tests and were given special permission to run light engine at 100 mph. On both occasions, the 'Deltics' were quickly returned to Finsbury Park after the tests.

On 15 January the up 'Flying Scotsman', diagrammed for a 'Deltic', departed from Edinburgh behind Class '47' 47533. By Doncaster, 47533 had begun to show signs of stress and was stopped, declared a failure, and removed to be replaced by 55004 *Queen's Own Highlander*. No 55004 made a spirited departure south and arrived at King's Cross only 40 mins late, after an exhilarating run.

Another unusual 'Deltic' event during January was the unexpected appearance of 55009 *Alycidon* at Stratford Depot on 19 January, while on 6 February it was an unexpected visitor to Aberdeen, arriving on a Class '47' diagram.

The gremlins were at work again on 1 February when 55003 *Meld* was at the head of the 12.00 King's Cross to Aberdeen. Trouble became apparent once the train was north of York, and *Meld* expired completely at Tollerton, to be rescued by Class '47' 47523 sent from York Depot. No 47523 eventually arrived at Newcastle with 55003 and train in tow, where both locomotives were replaced by another Class '47'.

On 29 March, there was engineering work on Selby swingbridge. One 'Deltic' diverted as a result was 55020 *Nimbus,* which travelled from Shaftsholme Junction, near Doncaster, via Knottingley, using freight-only lines to reach the Leeds to York line, continuing thence to Church Fenton and York. This detour had little effect on *Nimbus,* which was only 18 mins late into York. However, further north on the Edinburgh to Newcastle section the 08.00 Edinburgh to King's Cross, headed by 55014 *The Duke of Wellington's Regiment,* developed a transmission fault at Dunbar and had to proceed on one engine as far as Beal in Northumberland, where assistance was obtained from a Class '37' which had been summoned from Alnmouth. Progress then quickened, but only as far as Widdrington, where the 08.05 from Edinburgh, which had previously overtaken the King's Cross train at Beal, had failed in the forward section with its Class '45' in trouble. This train was then pushed to Morpeth, where the King's Cross train managed to get in front once more, proceeding to Newcastle 95 mins late. At Newcastle, 55012 *Crepello* took over and was some 2 hrs late upon arrival at York.

By April all the 'Deltics' had received the twin white spot type of headcode panel instead of the older type. During this period, 'Deltics' appeared to have a regular turn into Bradford Exchange with the Bradford portion of the 'Cornishman'. The 'Deltic' worked to Leeds on the down 'Yorkshire Pullman' before continuing thence to Bradford. One early black mark for the 'Deltics' on this diagram occurred on 26 April, when shortly before departure time with the 'Cornishman', 55020 *Nim-*

55008 The Green Howards has a well-earned rest at Finsbury Park Depot, displaying the twin-white-spot-type headcode panel which, along with 55022, she would retain up to withdrawal (being the only two 'Deltics' to do so) (D. Carter).

bus was declared a failure. Matters were, however, soon put right when 55005 *The Prince of Wales's Own Regiment of Yorkshire* replaced *Nimbus* for the short journey to Bradford.

Earlier in April, on the 9th, 55020 *Nimbus* was noted on a King's Cross to Cambridge diagram. Another unusual diagram to be 'Deltic'-worked was on 29 April when 55006 *The Fife and Forfar Yeomanry* put in an appearance at Huddersfield powering the York to Aberystwyth mail train. No 55006 worked as far as Stockport and returned on the balancing working. By that time this train had become quite accustomed to being hauled occasionally by a 'Deltic'.

During 1975, reports were made of 'Deltic' performance between Darlington and York. On four of these runs the time was less than 31 minutes between those two places, and the average speeds over the 28.2 miles from Danby Wiske to Beningborough were:

55016 — 100.6 mph (max speed reached 103 mph).

55003 — 101.0 mph (max speed reached 103 mph).

55010 — 104.3 mph (max speed reached 107 mph).

55003 — 103.7 mph (max speed reached 109 mph).

The above just goes to show that, in everyday service, the 'Deltics' were still capable of some fantastic speeds with apparently little effort.

York has always been one of my favourite cities, both from a railway and an historical point of view, and a visit on 21 June proved worthwhile, with almost every class of diesel-electric locomotive making an appearance including, of course, 'Deltics'. I recall Class '40' 40044 ticking over on York shed, making that unmistakable whistling sound, as 55002 *The King's Own Yorkshire Light Infantry* went powering past heading north for Newcastle. Other units noted that day were 55003/13/16/17 and 19, all well turned out externally and sounding mechanically excellent.

On 5 July, 55016 *Gordon Highlander* went into Doncaster Works for a general overhaul, the first of the class to be so treated. No 55016 did not emerge until 27 April 1976, after having been virtually rebuilt. Since then, only four other 'Deltics' were treated that way, Nos 55002/13/19 and 21. Further money and time could not be allowed for the rest of the class to be dealt with in this way so late in their careers, with the advent of the HST operation just around the corner. Nos 55016 and 55019 received more attention than the other three; rewiring and stripping down to check the condition of the inner body skins were just two of the major jobs undertaken during their overhauls.

August saw two different 'Deltics' succumb to failure. On the 5th, 55019 was hauling the 16.00 King's Cross to Edinburgh when, upon arrival at York, she had to be removed in favour of a Class '47'. On the 12th trouble struck again, when about two miles south of Newcastle 55019 again became a failure. After about 65 mins the train (the 12.10

55006 The Fife and Forfar Yeomanry *streaks past Castle Hill Junction, Northallerton, on 2 August 1975 heading a down Edinburgh express. (The line curving away to the right is the freight-only line to Redmire)* (N. Skinner).

A smart-looking 55008 The Green Howards *stands at Peterborough North awaiting departure with a down train* (D. Carter Collection)

'Aberdonian') was on the move again, the following 'Deltic'-hauled train giving it a push in the rear. This procession negotiated the curves on to the King Edward Bridge and into Newcastle Central Station without much trouble, but with a great deal of hand-signalling from the cab of 55019. The third incident occurred at York again on the 27th, when 55014 *The Duke of Wellington's Regiment* failed whilst working the 'Tees-Tyne Pullman'. After a 20 mins' wait the train departed behind Class '47' 47549.

On 27 September, 55022 was in trouble when it was removed from the 09.00 King's Cross to Newcastle at Doncaster, where Class '47' 47224 took over and departed one hour late.

The autumn showed no change in the sightings of 'Deltics' and no retrograde steps in their performance, although some members of the class were beginning to look decidedly grubby, though this was probably due to sustained high-speed running in bad weather rather than lack of care. A day at Gateshead that autumn provided the sight of units 55002/3/6/10/13/15 and 22.

The beginning of October was a bad time for 55013 *The Black Watch.* On the 6th the up 'Hull Pullman' made an unscheduled stop at Peterborough, where Class '25' 25099 was attached for the rest of the run to King's Cross due to partial loss of power on 55013. The pair arrived in London some 40 mins late. The next day, 55013 was apparently in no better condition, when it again had to take assistance after suffering another partial engine failure at Doncaster whilst heading the 07.20 Bradford to King's Cross. This time Class '31' 31250 was attached as pilot but the train lost time en route, rarely exceeding 60 mph, and arrival was 37 mins late into King's Cross.

A better time was had five days later on 12 October when pomp and glory was lavished upon 55003 *Meld* when she was used to haul a special from Paddington to Cardiff and return. What a sight and sound *Meld* must have made on that return journey climbing out of the Severn Tunnel and on up Patchway Bank! According to witnesses aboard the train *Meld* performed admirably. This special was only one of the first of many in the future, proving the high esteem and affection with which these 'kings' of diesels were, and still are, held.

The only other information to come my way during the latter part of 1975 was bad news for 55006 *The Fife and Forfar Yeomanry*. Standing at Edinburgh Waverley Station on 30 November awaiting departure with the 16.00 Edinburgh to King's Cross train, a fire broke out inside the locomotive. No 55006 was quickly uncoupled and removed to a suitable siding by the station pilot where the local fire brigade could extinguish the fire. Eventually the train departed 38 mins late behind 55013 *The Black Watch* and 55006 was towed away to Haymarket Depot.

1976

'...all the class had well cleared the two million miles mark...'

The year started with the regular use of 'Deltics' on the Hull to Doncaster line, the 03.56 from Doncaster and the 06.45 up 'Hull Pullman' being among the first turns to see their use.

One event which occurred during January, and which showed a ray of hope for a 'Deltic' to slip into immortality, took place on the 24th when the 'Deltic' Society was formed with the aim of preserving a 'Deltic' on withdrawal. However, this the first attempt to secure one of the locomotives was dissolved on 7 August. This decision was taken after a letter was received from the Keeper of the National Railway Museum at York advising that negotiations between British Rail and the National Railway Museum were in an advanced state whereby on withdrawal, possibly in the 1980s, a 'Deltic' would be put on display at York. Little did we know at that time that the 'Deltic' in question would be 55002 *The King's Own Yorkshire Light Infantry* and that another band of enthusiasts known as the 'Deltic' Preservation Society would be formed to preserve a working example — but more of that later.

The National Railway Museum's eventual choice, 55002 The King's Own Yorkshire Light Infantry, *heads towards Haughton Road bridge, Darlington, on a down train for Edinburgh* (H. Watson).

Otherwise the first two months of 1976 slipped by without incident, but this changed during March when, due to a drivers' dispute, 'Deltics' 55005 *The Prince of Wales's Own Regiment of Yorkshire* and 55007 *Pinza* were used on the Cleethorpes services — 55007 on the 12.20 down and the 17.42 return on 10 March and 55005 on the same services the following day.

Up until March, British Rail had kept the individual mileage records of each 'Deltic' since new, but after the 27th they considered this practice unnecessary and stopped it. At that time, the 22 'Deltics' had amassed a total of 54,705,000 miles, the highest mileage for an individual unit being that of 55010 *The King's Own Scottish Borderer* with 2,535,411 miles, closely followed by 55006 *The Fife and Forfar Yeomanry* with 2,534,563 miles. No 55009 *Alycidon* had been the last 'Deltic' to reach 2,000,000 miles in October 1974.

During 1976 the 'Deltics' began to appear with their headcode panels completely blanked off, except for two separate circular lights peering through the now completely yellow nose. No 55016 *Gordon Highlander* was the first to be so treated, and was noted in this guise outside Doncaster Works on 11 April.

In their main-line careers the 'Deltics' were in fact to see over 200 modifications to their design which, in no small way, contributed to the high, trouble-free (at times) mileages they attained; by 1976, when all the class had well cleared the two million miles mark, this was still reflected in their everyday performance. A run recorded during 1976 by O. S. Nock showed what a 'Deltic' could do between Newcastle and Edinburgh on the Saturday 12-coach down 'Flying Scotsman'. Altogether the train weighed some 445 tons full and was hauled by 55013 *The Black Watch*. It should be noted that even in 1976 this stretch of the East Coast Main Line still had it old hindrances, although some of the regular speed restrictions had been raised a little, such as 47 mph at Morpeth, 69 mph at Alnmouth, 50 mph at Berwick and 62 mph at Dunbar. It was, in fact, only along the Northumberland coastal strip north of

55004 Queen's Own Highlander *stands on the 'lawn' at Doncaster Works, fitted with plated-over headcode panels with two lights inserted* (D. Carter).

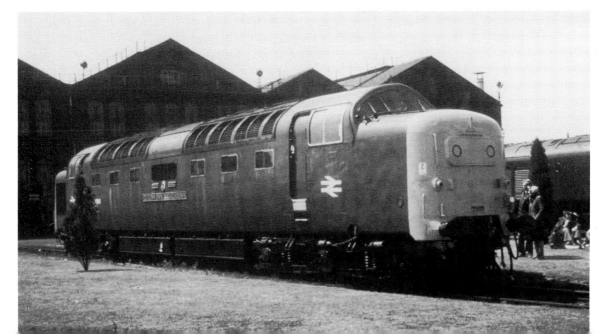

*55013 The Black Watch,
hero of the run described here,
passes light engine through
York Station* (D. Carter).

Little Mill that any real speeding by 55013 could be made, otherwise the maximum then was around 90 mph.

Nonetheless, 55013 passed Longhirst at 85 mph, reached 92 mph at Acklington, and then eased down to the stipulated 69 mph through Alnmouth. Once on the coastal racing stretch, 55013 began to fly, with 91 mph by Chathill, 98-96 mph at Belford and the maximum of 102 mph passing Beal, before easing to 90 mph at Scremerston, and down to 50 mph for the restriction through Berwick. Once north of the Border, 55013 cleared Cockburnspath at 84 mph and reached 87 mph at East Linton, after being slowed to 62 mph for the Dunbar restriction. The outcome was that although 55013 left Newcastle on time, it reached Edinburgh 7.5 mins early.

It seems a shame that after telling of such a fine run it has to be reported that on 17 April 55013 failed at York with a fault on one engine; two fitters could not diagnose the problem, so Class '08' 08540 removed 55013 to the depot. No 47518 eventually took the train away some 30 mins late. Two days later, the 08.50 Aberdeen to King's Cross arrived at York behind 55021 *Argyll and Sutherland Highlander,* again running on one engine and replaced by Class '47' 47523. Such were the penalties to be paid for such arduous high-speed running for prolonged hours on end, of which the 'Deltics' really proved themselves capable, being virtually trouble-free compared with certain other classes.

It was probably the prolonged hours in service that contributed to a sight that met my eyes on 5 May at Gateshead Depot, when 55009 *Alycidon* appeared in a truly sad state, being absolutely filthy and unkempt — definitely no credit to Finsbury Park Depot. Its BR logo was scratched away in places, as was its number, and it was on that occasion that I first noticed on a 'Deltic' a kind of rippled effect on the bodyside panels, which I was told later was the result of metal fatigue over the years, but whether this is correct or not I do not know. However, I do not suppose that *Alycidon* was in that condition for very long, as Finsbury Park always took a pride in the appearance of their 'Deltics' in general, as was apparent in later years.

During the summer, the 'Deltics' became quite commonplace on the Cleethorpes to London services. For example, on 24 June 55007 *Pinza* was seen at the head of the 12.20 from King's Cross and the 17.42 return, while 15 September saw 55009 *Alycidon* on the 08.30 from King's Cross returning south on the 12.56 train.

Towards the latter half of the year, although still not relegated by the HSTs, it was strange to hear of the various duties on which the 'Deltics' were being used, duties that even a Class '40' or '46' would have found degrading, and one began to wonder just what would become of these proud racehorses of the East Coast Main Line after the advent of HST operation — and how little we knew of what exactly was to come! On 29 November, the Edinburgh district found itself short of serviceable diesel multiple units, so much so that 55020 *Nimbus* was

55009 Alycidon *arrives on Gateshead Depot on 5 May 1976 in a rather dirty state, apart from the cleaned yellow ends* (H. Watson).

55014 The Duke of
Wellington's Regiment, *the
'Deltic' involved in the Selby
failure, seen here in better times
awaiting departure from
Huntingdon* (D. Carter).

turned out to work the 6-coach 07.51 Falkirk Grahamstown to Edinburgh Waverley. On 1 December, 55006 *The Fife and Forfar Yeomanry* was also used on this mundane turn and later, on 9 December 55019 *Royal Highland Fusilier*.

Another tale of woe closed the year when, on 21 December, the 09.20 Newcastle to King's Cross rolled into Doncaster some 55 mins late with Class '31' 31131 towing defective 'Deltic' 55014 *The Duke of Wellington's Regiment* and train which had expired at Selby Canal Junction. At Doncaster both locomotives were removed in favour of Class '47' 47220, which put up a swift run to London.

The year came to an end with the assurance that at least one production 'Deltic' was to be preserved for posterity, a message which gladdened the heart of every 'Deltic' enthusiast.

1977

'...'Deltic' sightings north of York were becoming noticeably fewer.'

The dawning of 1977 still saw the 'Deltics' as the East Coast Main Line's front-line power, but even though the HST still had not stolen the scene, 'Deltic' sightings north of York were becoming noticeably fewer. Many of their rostered duties were being worked by Class '47's and two that I remember quite clearly deputizing on 'Deltic' diagrams during this period were 47421 and 47518. The reason for this state of affairs was most probably the lack of spare parts at Doncaster Works, because at around this time 'Deltics' were certainly not going in and out of Doncaster Works as rapidly as in the past. A visit to the Newcastle area during the early part of the year was hardly worthwhile, with no 'Deltics' at Gateshead shed and only two (55016 and 55019) seen passing through on the main line. A day at Darlington later in the spring proved no bet-

55019 Royal Highland Fusilier *heads the up 'Flying Scotsman' past King Edward Bridge Junction, Gateshead, on 26 March 1977, one of only two 'Deltics' noted on main-line service that day during a seven-hour period* (H. Watson).

55022 Royal Scots Grey receives a tumultuous 'send-off' from Edinburgh Waverley Station on the inaugural 'Silver Jubilee' for King's Cross, 8 June 1977 (D. Carter).

ter, with only 55008 and 55013 being noted in a five-hour period on 4 April (even the up 'Flying Scotsman' had a Class '47' in charge!). This kind of sporadic 'Deltic' appearance went on throughout 1977; some days almost nothing was noted and on others sightings were more numerous, although never anywhere near the level of the mid to late 'sixties.

Personally, next to the 'Deltics' my favourite class of diesel is the Class '50', but if there was a gold medal to be awarded it must go to the Class '47's, which on occasions during the late 'seventies surely surpassed themselves when, time and time again, they so admirably deputized for 'Deltics', even on such trains as the 'Flying Scotsman', 'Talisman' and 'Silver Jubilee', mostly putting up the most fantastic performances.

One strange side-effect of this frequent absence of 'Deltics' from their normal turns on the East Coast Main Line was that they were still to be seen on less exacting duties away from the main line. The use of 'Deltics' on these mundane duties seemed, to the enthusiast, ridiculous! The '47's, which at that time were being used on 'Deltic' turns, could have been better utilized, making the 'Deltics' available for the job for which they were intended. For instance, on 2 February 55016 *Gordon Highlander* arrived at Derby with Class '46' 46032 in tow. No 55016 then returned north almost immediately after disposing of its load. Two other instances were on 11 June when 55018 *Ballymoss* was used on the 17.37 Cleethorpes to King's Cross, and 17 June when 55020 *Nimbus* was a most unusual sight at Brighouse heading the Huddersfield and Halifax portion of the 18.04 from King's Cross. No doubt BR had good reason for the use of 'Deltics' in this manner.

On a happier note, Eastern Region celebrated the Queen's 25-year reign on 8 June by introducing a named train, the 'Silver Jubilee'. This service was, if at all possible, to be exclusively 'Deltic'-hauled and ran between King's Cross and Edinburgh, leaving Edinburgh on the inaugural day at 15.00 for King's Cross headed by an immaculate 55022 *Royal Scots Grey*. The down departure was 07.45 from King's Cross. Unfortunately, this service only ran until 5 May 1978.

The 'Aberdonian' was in trouble on 21 June when 55021 *Argyll and Sutherland Highlander* limped into Peterborough with one engine out of action. Class '40' 40085 was quickly attached as pilot but arrival at King's Cross was 48 mins late. Another 'Deltic' in trouble on 30 June was *Ballymoss* (55018), which developed engine trouble north of York on the down 'Silver Jubilee'. Class '40' 40074 was detached from a van train and piloted the ailing 'Deltic' as far as Newcastle, where both locomotives were relieved by Class '47' 47550. The '47' eventually departed for Edinburgh 49 mins late. No 40074 then towed 55018, still bearing the 'Silver Jubilee' headboard, away towards Gateshead Depot.

A happier occasion was 30 June at York when a plaque was unveiled to commemorate the centenary of the station. In celebration, some steam engines were on exhibition in the station and on the following Sunday an HST set and 'Deltic' 55013 *The Black Watch* were made available for filming purposes.

55014 The Duke of Wellington's Regiment accelerates away from Platform 1 at Darlington Bank Top on the 'Silver Jubilee', complete with headboard, during 1977 (D. Carter).

Class '47' 47403 arrives at Darlington Bank Top deputizing for a 'Deltic' on an up Edinburgh to King's Cross service (H. Watson).

July was distinguished by the appearance of two 'Deltics' on the Hellifield to Carnforth line, both on specials. The first was on the 10th with 55007 *Pinza*, whilst a fortnight later 55003 *Meld* was the celebrity.

During two weekends in September, East Coast Main Line trains were diverted via Knottingley and the Askern branch to reach Doncaster. On 17-18 September, trains on the Doncaster to York section were routed via Church Fenton and Knottingley, following a derailment at Selby, and the following weekend bridge works on the Doncaster to Leeds line caused all trains to run via Featherstone and Knottingley. Five 'Deltics' (55002/4/10/11 and 15) were observed on the second weekend.

On 24 September, 55012 *Crepello* was chosen to work north out of King's Cross on an excursion entitled 'Deltic Pictorial Railtour'. It really *was* a picture to see 55012 in pristine condition departing with the stock of the 'Silver Jubilee' and, as a bonus, adorned with the 'Silver Jubilee' headboard.

Unofficial industrial action by maintenance staff resulted in the sudden disappearance of 'Deltics' from East Coast Main Line workings during the week commencing 17 October. This arose from concern over the future of Finsbury Park Depot when HST services commenced using the new Bounds Green Depot. As a result the 'Deltics' were 'blacked' by the staff who carried out their routine maintenance, and by 20 October three of the class were out of action at York, four at Gateshead and an unknown number at Finsbury Park. The resultant shortage of motive power fitted with electric train heating and air-conditioning equipment caused Eastern Region to commandeer all available locomotives fitted with such equipment until the dispute was over; it was finally settled on 21 October.

During, and for a short time after, the 'Deltic' dispute, defects started to show up in the other classes that had been involved in the swap-round to cover the 'Deltic' diagrams. The class which had taken the heaviest brunt of the 'stand-in' work was '47', many members of which in particular became failures, probably due to abnormally intensive use at speeds to which these locomotives were not normally accustomed for such prolonged periods. One '47' noted on several occasions during this period was 47421 which, for some reason or other, I have always had an affection towards, probably because it was Gatehead-based at the time and always seemed to be fairly clean externally for a Gateshead locomotive!

In late November, the 'Deltics' again began to turn up on a number of workings to Cleethorpes. On the 23rd, for instance, 55015 *Tulyar* was seen at the head of the 12.20 from King's Cross and the 17.37 return working. Next day even the use of super-power in the form of 55014 *The Duke of Wellington's Regiment* failed to prevent the 08.25 from King's Cross running one hour late. This train was in fact eventually terminated at Barnetby and passengers were transferred to a local train to complete their journey. Later that day 55020 *Nimbus* arrived safely at Cleethorpes on the 12.20 from King's Cross and returned to the capital on the 17.37.

Nimbus was again in the news on 25 November when she failed near Welwyn on the 14.00 King's Cross to Aberdeen, and was eventually stopped at Hitchin. It then struggled forward to Peterborough on one engine, arriving there 45 mins late. The only replacement available was 47263, which was not fitted with electric train heating equipment but had to be used, eventually departing one hour late. Nearly two weeks later, on 7 December, Class '46' 46029 was noted with 'Deltics' 55005 and 55007 in tow heading south through Darlington, probably on their way from Gateshead to Doncaster Works for repairs. *Nimbus* turned up yet again during late December when it was sent to Stratford Depot for repairs to a bogie defect.

On 23 December, a train which in future years was to see regular 'Deltic' haulage, the 07.25 Plymouth to Edinburgh, rolled into Newcastle behind 55016 *Gordon Highlander,* which had taken over at York. On the same day, 55005 *The Prince of Wales's Own Regiment of Yorkshire* arrived at King Edward Bridge Junction on the down 'Flying Scotsman' some 10 mins early and, after being stopped on the bridge itself, was allowed into Newcastle Central still 2 mins early.

With the end of 1977 came the end of the last full year in which the 'Deltics' would see use on such trains as the 'Flying Scotsman' for 1978 was to see the advent of the HST in revenue-earning service on a large scale. This sad period is always reflected in my memory by the sight of 55007 *Pinza* tearing out of Darlington Bank Top Station on 5 November

Left *55012* Crepello *on the up 'Flying Scotsman' overtakes Class '50' 50016* Barham *on the Doncaster Works test train* (H. Watson).

Below left *Tyneside's Gateshead Depot during 1977. Locomotives (left to right) are 46032, 55017* The Durham Light Infantry, *55021* Argyll and Sutherland Highlander, *03056 and 31418* (H. Watson).

past the DMU Depot heading north in true 'Deltic' style and passing 55006 *The Fife and Forfar Yeomanry* drifting in from the north. Alas, I did not have my camera with me to record this event.

Speaking of photographs, on 12 December I got the opportunity to take one of my most treasured pictures at King Edward Bridge Junction, Gateshead. The Doncaster test train ran as far as Newcastle and returned to Doncaster behind any class of locomotive that had been outshopped that day. As luck would have it, that particular day it was Class '50' 50016 *Barham* in ex works condition. After running around its train in Central Station, it proceeded slowly south out on to King Edward Bridge towards me as 55012 *Crepello* on the up 'Scotsman' began to overtake. There was just enough time for me to take a shot of them both coming off the bridge, my two favourite classes running neck and neck — a truly wonderful sight!

That day was my last visit to Tyneside before the HST took full control of the top link duties, so I was very pleased when it turned out to be one of the better days for seeing 'Deltics'. Although not as good as I would have liked, it was still worthwhile with 55003/10/12/13 and 19 coming my way. No 55013 was seen standing at the rear of Gateshead Depot in the company of 37032, but in the late afternoon was seen storming south with a dead Class '47' in tow and, as they both disappeared towards Bensham, so did my 'Deltic' adventures for 1977.

1978

'...during May, more 'Deltic' duties were turned over to HSTs.'

55003 Meld *at Bristol Temple Meads while heading the 'Deltic Ranger' rail tour to Devon on 5 March 1978* (D. Carter).

The year started on a friendly note for the 'Deltics' when, on 29 January, 55018 *Ballymoss* was used by Western Region to power an RPPR special from Paddington to Treherbert as far as Cardiff. The train, the 'Deltic Dragon' tour, worked to Wales via Evesham and Gloucester and returned to Paddington by the more usual route of Newport, Severn Tunnel Junction and Swindon.

On 19 February, *Ballymoss* was again loaned to Western Region for the 'Deltic Ranger' tour from Paddington to Devon. This special, unfortunately, had to be terminated at Bristol because of appalling weather conditions further west. Fortunately, the weather was much improved at

the time of the second attempt on 5 March when 55003 *Meld* was used and made a creditable run from Paddington to Paignton and back.

Meanwhile, back on the East Coast Main Line, services had been delayed on 13 February when 55010 *The King's Own Scottish Borderer* failed whilst heading the 08.30 Newcastle to King's Cross. Class '31' 31301 was summoned to assist 55010, and was noted passing Peterborough more than an hour late. A week earlier, on the 6th, 55008 *The Green Howards* expired at Grantham and arrived at Doncaster towed by 47037. Here both locomotives were quickly removed and the train departed 25 mins late behind 55007 *Pinza*.

The next month, on 26 March, 55007 *Pinza* was brought back into the limelight when, impeccably turned out, she hauled a DA/AD & EG special train 'The Man of Kent', which ran from Victoria and visited all three divisions of the Southern Region.

Perhaps the first indication of the reality of the end of the 'Deltics' occurred at 07.45 on 20 March when an HST took over the first formerly 'Deltic' rostered duty. My first personal experience of these developments was on 4 April when, to my dismay, most of the 'Deltic' turns passing through Darlington that day had been turned over to HST operation, and salt was really rubbed into the wound when, at 10.00, 47525 rolled into Bank Top on a 'Deltic' turn for King's Cross. In fact, the only 'Deltic' I noted that day up to 12.30 was 55017 *The Durham Light Infantry*. No 55002 *The King's Own Yorkshire Light Infantry* was the one unit that I saw on numerous occasions around this time; for a short while it was the only 'Deltic' I saw on my frequent, but short, visits to Darlington and Ferryhill — but oh, what a state she was in externally, not

The infiltrator — the brand new HST power car from set 254020 at York on 20 August 1978 (H. Watson).

helped by the weather prevailing at the time!

The trend continued — during May, more 'Deltic' duties were turned over to HSTs. The 'Deltics' thus displaced took up other duties which, at that time, were not 'Deltic' diagrammed. Some of these duties were the heavy overnight sleeper services which, in turn, released Class '47's for other duties. The last down weekday 'Flying Scotsman' to be 'Deltic' hauled rolled into Newcastle on 6 May headed by 55010 *The King's Own Scottish Borderer,* marking the end of an era. The previous day had been the last day of service for the 'Yorkshire Pullman' and 'Hull Pullman' trains. 'Deltics' were used on both up 'Pullmans' that day — 55002 on the 'Yorkshire' coming up from passing Grantham in 74 mins.

Almost immediately, the redundant 'Deltics' began to appear on some most unusual duties. On the fateful 6 May itself, the normally quiet station at Spalding received an additional 12,000 passengers as visitors flocked to the Annual Flower Festival. In addition to the unusual arrival of Class '33' 33034 from the Southern Region, other unusual visitors were 55016 *Gordon Highlander* on a train from Newcastle and 55011 *The Royal Northumberland Fusiliers* on a train from King's Cross. The day before, 55016 *Gordon Highlander* was turned out to work, of all

Although during daytime in 1978 the 'Deltics' were scarce north of York, further south it was different — seen here in King's Cross Fuelling Yard are 55021 Argyll and Sutherland Highlander *and 55022* Royal Scots Grey *(D. Carter Collection).*

things, the 17.10 Newcastle to Hexham and the 18.10 return, although
two days previously, on the 3rd, matters had been a shade better when
55018 *Ballymoss* was utilized on the 17.55 Edinburgh to Leeds.

By contrast, on 20 May, Finsbury Park Depot turned out an impeccable 55012 *Crepello* to work a special, 'The Thames-Forth Express',
from London to Edinburgh and return, taking in parts of the old
Midland route.

At the beginning of May there was an industrial dispute at Doncaster works which delayed the return to traffic of many locomotives
fitted with electric train heating equipment, including the 'Deltics';
however, by this time, due to the introduction of the HST units, perhaps
the action did not have the impact as in the past. In fact, it was reported
that during April only five 'Deltics' were in traffic running on two
engines, all others being in use on one engine only or awaiting entry into
Doncaster Works. At that time, nine 'Deltics' and several Class '50's
were in the works but no-one at the time knew for how long because of
the dispute. Meanwhile, up and down the East Coast Main Line the
situation, as already mentioned, had been eased because of the HST introduction, but even so some 'Deltic' diagrams had to be worked by the

versatile Class '47's and the sight of a 'Deltic' north of York during the daytime had become comparatively rare.

One very sad sign of the times was that during virtually the whole of April 55020 *Nimbus*, after failing in the Tyneside area, was dumped at the rear of Gateshead Depot before being towed away to Doncaster Works, whence she was destined never again to emerge into traffic. Instead, she was mechanically cannibalized to get other members of the class back into service. Two 'Deltics' to re-enter service shortly after this were 55008 *The Green Howards* and 55001 *St Paddy*, both of which had, most probably, used parts from *Nimbus*. Alas, all did not go well with *St Paddy*, for not long afterwards she also returned to the works to suffer the same fate as *Nimbus*.

So, it appeared that within days of the advent of the HST, the first 'Deltic' withdrawal seemed imminent, although by mid-summer 1979, 55020 was still languishing inside Doncaster Works, partly cannibalized but still not officially withdrawn; it still seemed possible that when spares became more readily available *Nimbus* might run once again, but as already stated this was not to be.

The month of June arrived and, although the class was starting to feature more strongly on East Coast Main Line services, one or two members were still finding their way on to other duties. On 5 June, 55018 *Ballymoss* hauled the 08.25 King's Cross to Cleethorpes and the 13.18 return, and the next day found 55021 *Argyll and Sutherland Highlander* on the 07.08 Peterborough to King's Cross commuter train. On the 7th, an unusual combination turned up at King's Cross on the 'Aberdonian' when 55005 *The Prince of Wales's Own Regiment of Yorkshire* arrived with 31418 as pilot, having apparently suffered engine trouble further north.

As more HST units entered service during July, the 'Deltics' began to be used quite frequently on the 21.50 York to Shrewsbury mail train as far as Stockport and return, a diagram on which they had performed

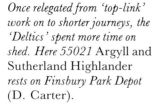

Once relegated from 'top-link' work on to shorter journeys, the 'Deltics' spent more time on shed. Here 55021 Argyll and Sutherland Highlander *rests on Finsbury Park Depot* (D. Carter).

admirably in the past from time to time. The first 'Deltic' noted on this train was 55017 *The Durham Light Infantry* on 5 July, followed by 55014 *The Duke of Wellington's Regiment* on the 19th and 55021 *Argyll and Sutherland Highlander* on the 26th.

On 15 July 55018 *Ballymoss* found itself in trouble with a hot axlebox while heading the 18.04 King's Cross to Bradford. The fault occurred south of Peterborough and the luckless *Ballymoss* was promptly removed at North Station. The only locomotive available was Class '31' 31195, which took the train away north; *Ballymoss* later cautiously returned to Finsbury Park light engine.

Later in the month, on the 23rd, another excursion starring a 'Deltic', sponsored by British Rail and called 'The Merrymaker', departed from Chesterfield headed by an immaculate 55003 *Meld*. The special travelled by way of Sheffield to reach Carlisle, its destination, and also featured a visit to 'Steamtown', Carnforth, en route. The next month, on 13 August, there was yet another excursion headed by a Finsbury Park 'Deltic'. This time it was 55015 *Tulyar,* which was chosen to haul a train from King's Cross to Skegness throughout, via Lincoln on the outward trip.

By and large, the summer of 1978 had found the 'Deltics' in a sad situation, except for the odd call for a better-conditioned member of the class to haul a special excursion, and the autumn was not to be any brighter. In fact, 'Deltics' entering Doncaster Works towards the latter part of the year were doing so for far longer periods than previously. For instance, 55001 *St Paddy* was in the works for over five months before being returned to traffic. 55004 *Queen's Own Highlander* also had a lengthy sojourn; it arrived in the works on 28 April and was still there by mid-August. Lack of spare parts was understood to be the major factor causing the detention of the locomotives.

Although now at the beginning of their 'twilight years', with seemingly everything set against them, the 'Deltics', already a legend in their

Sad situation, sad condition — 55015 Tulyar *stands at Peterborough North on a down express* (D. Carter).

own time, began to develop almost individual personalities, with enthusiasts travelling from far and wide to pay homage to these magnificent machines. In their last few years I met an enthusiast from Devon, who would never have thought of heading north-east to see a Gresley 'Pacific' when he could have stayed at home to see 'Kings' or 'Castles', but thought nothing of travelling hundreds of miles to see and hear a 'Deltic' in full flight. The strange thing was that, during my travels, by far the most popular with the enthusiast in general seemed to be the 'racehorses', or London-based 'Deltics', which, by coincidence, always seemed to be at the head of the earlier specially-chartered excursions. This factor may have been borne out of the individual popularity of the 'racehorses' or it may have been their geographical allocation in relation to the starting point of most of the excursions, as was the case on 3 September when a natural choice for an excursion from King's Cross to Lowestoft and return was 55015 *Tulyar*. Of course, it was not only the 'racehorses' which were chosen for an excursion or a special run out of King's Cross; on 30 September, 55013 *The Black Watch* had the privilege of working the last down 'Aberdonian'.

On 2 October more HST units entered service, rendering still more previous 'Deltic' turns redundant. After this date, the favourite turns for the 'Deltics' became the Cleethorpes trains, along with the Hull expresses and the Leeds and York semi-fasts, all from King's Cross. Further north, and my own personal favourite 'Deltic' turn, was the Edinburgh to Plymouth train as far as York, and the down balancing working the same day, although gladly this did not always feature the same 'Deltic' both ways. It was on these services and others that 'Deltics' were to end their days.

During the late 1970s, Doncaster took over the overhaul of the Class '50' diesel-electrics, then working over the main lines of the Western Region. One favourite way of getting them to and from Doncaster was to sometimes utilize them on the north-east to south-west services to and from York. Once at York, the Class '50' would await a suitable path, then head off for Doncaster or vice versa. One such occasion was 19 September when 50046 wanted a path from Doncaster to York. Instead of running light, it was coupled ahead of 55002 *The King's Own Yorkshire Light Infantry* on an express from King's Cross to the north and detached at York in readiness for its journey south-west; the 'Deltic', of course, continued on its journey north.

Another service which was linked to Doncaster Works by way of being used for the running-in of locomotives was the 09.30 King's Cross to Newcastle which, besides the occasional Class '50' saw on 24 October Class '47' 47521 piloted by ex-works 55010 *The King's Own Scottish Borderer*. Three days later, 55012 *Crepello* was noted in ex-works condition on an Edinburgh train.

To indicate the depths to which the 'Deltics' had sunk in their working lives by late 1978, it is best to cite an instance. The 07.28 Stamford to Peterborough service during that autumn reverted to locomotive haulage on weekdays, the DMU displaced from this working being used to work a Peterborough to Grantham connecting service. This revised service was operated while work continued on the lowering of tracks in Stoke and Peascliffe Tunnels. A Class '31' usually worked the train, running as empty stock to Stamford. On arrival at Peterborough it formed the 07.58 to King's Cross, and on 26 October the locomotive rostered to this train arrived at Stamford in the shape of 'Deltic' 55022 *Royal Scots Grey,* and worked the whole diagram through to King's Cross. Although this was not a regular 'Deltic' turn, it shows how, around this time, a 'Deltic' could even be spared to deputize for a Class '31'.

York Station soon became one of the best outposts for enthusiasts living north of that city to see 'Deltics' in their last years. On one particular day in the autumn of 1978 I was treated to the sight of seven 'Deltics'. First to arrive was 55019 *Royal Highland Fusilier,* in fair external condition, on a train from the north to King's Cross. Later, 55021 *Argyll and Sutherland Highlander* arrived on an Edinburgh to London train, followed by 55013 *The Black Watch,* also heading south. Both these 'Deltics' were in fine external condition, a credit to Haymarket Depot. Next to arrive from the north was 55008 *The Green Howards,* not long out of Doncaster Works and now sounding in trouble. As she came to a stop in the station, the driver immediately stopped the engines, summoned a fitter and disappeared into the cavernous engine compartment to rectify the fault. Meanwhile, Class '40' 40050 came whistling past and stopped on an adjacent road, a possible deputy for the ailing 'Deltic'. After a while, human endurance and skill won the day. No 55008 burst into life and departed south in great haste, as though nothing had been wrong, its engine being heard long after it had disappeared out of sight towards Dringhouses. After this, a disappointed 40050 retreated back towards the depot, being cheated of a chance to show its paces.

55008 The Green Howards, *after emergency repairs, awaits departure from York* (H. Watson).

A very rare spectacle! The quickest way to get 37009 from Darlington to Berwick-upon-Tweed on 19 September 1978 was to attach it in front of 55008 The Green Howards *on the 05.50 King's Cross to Aberdeen, seen here passing Ferryhill, Co Durham (H. Watson).*

Not long afterwards, 55018 *Ballymoss* arrived on a semi-fast from London in nice condition and retired to the depot after disposing of its stock. Next came 55012 *Crepello* on a train from King's Cross to the north — and what an exit she made with her heavy train away round that curve to the north out of York Station! By late afternoon, just as I was myself ready to depart for home, I noted my seventh 'Deltic' — 55009 *Alycidon*.

At around this time, on 19 September I witnessed and photographed 55008 *The Green Howards* at Ferryhill, Co Durham being piloted by 37009 on the 05.50 King's Cross-Aberdeen — a truly rare spectacle, and indicative of a year that was to come to an end with the 'Deltics' in a really precarious position. Would British Rail now call it a day for these unique but expensive-to-maintain locomotives — or would better ways be found to employ them, at least for a few years?

1979

'...the official withdrawal date for the class was drawing nearer...'

The new year came in as the old had ended, with a cloud hanging over the 'Deltics'; they continued to plod on with the Cleethorpes, Hull and York trains and, of course, the overnight sleeper trains. Although they might have been more common north of York on these nocturnal services, during daylight they were certainly becoming scarce. In fact, for a time, 55002 *The King's Own Yorkshire Light Infantry*, 55005 *The Prince Of Wales's Own Regiment of Yorkshire* and 55014 *The Duke of Wellington's Regiment* were the only 'Deltics' I noted working north of York although, of course, others would have been at work during the hours of darkness. Two others also popular at that time were 55022 *Royal Scots Grey* and the beautiful 55021 *Argyll and Sutherland Highlander* (what a name!). Why was it that 55021 always sounded so sweet and, ninety-nine times out of a hundred, looked so good externally? I often wondered if there was someone up at Haymarket who gave her special attention — if so, many thanks!

Besides their now regular employment on the more secondary East Coast trains, a Sunday morning York to Darlington parcels working became a regular 'Deltic' duty for a while. This parcels train, which usually had a minimal number of vehicles, became a kind of bonus for the Darlington-based 'Deltic' enthusiast. On one such parcels train, comprising only three vans, 55016 *Gordon Highlander* was noted at York on 7 January.

One exceptional working for a 'Deltic' occurred due to bad weather on 17 February when a two-car DMU working was replaced by 55011 *The Royal Northumberland Fusiliers* with two Mk I coaches! Such was the mediocre work these locomotives were, at that time, facing, but just how long could it last?

Until 17 March the three main East Coast route tunnel engineering works at Stoke, Peascliffe and Penmanshiel had continued unabated. On that date, at Penmanshiel Tunnel between Berwick and Dunbar in Scotland, disaster struck when a section of the tunnel collapsed, blocking the East Coast Main Line to the north and south completely and, sadly,

During diversions from the East Coast Main Line, 55009 Alycidon departs from Stockton-on-Tees with an up express (D. Carter).

killing two workmen who were buried, never to be found. This resulted in Anglo-Scottish services being diverted via the Tyne Valley, Carlisle and Carstairs, then across to Edinburgh. This, of course, resulted in all the familiar East Coast classes becoming common at Carlisle, including the 'Deltics'.

To compound the problems on the already crippled East Coast Main Line, a landslip occurred after heavy rain near Relly Mill Junction south of Durham on 30 March. This resulted in trains being diverted from the East Coast Main Line at Northallerton and reaching Newcastle via the coast route through Stockton, Hartlepool and Sunderland, until a single track was re-opened. However, on 4 April there were delays of more than three hours when this single section was blocked by the locomotive of a ballast train which broke down whilst going to repair the breach.

Until the main line could be returned to normal, it was a marvel of operation on the secondary coast route, especially at Stockton-on-Tees, where heavy coal, chemical tanker and Consett trains, as well as the local commuter trains and emergency shuttle services from Darlington, had to be slipped in with the normal freight and express passenger trains now diverted from the main line. I do not think this coastal route had seen such a density of traffic before or since. Of course, the 'Deltics' were included in the steady flow of traffic (including my favourite, *Pinza*) but alas they were few and far between.

Further south, on 21 February, a DMU failure at Peterborough resulted in 55019 *Royal Highland Fusilier* being used on the 13.57 Peterborough to Leicester and the 15.23 return, while earlier, on 27 January, 55002 *The King's Own Yorkshire Light Infantry* was noted passing Castlecary in charge of the 13.44 Glasgow to Edinburgh van train, which comprised only three vehicles; like Eastern Region, Scottish Region was having difficulty in finding suitable employment for the 'Deltics'. Even towards the summer, things had not improved. The 'Deltics' based at Haymarket and Gateshead by then did not have much work to do because the East Coast Main Line had its full quota of HSTs, so the use of 'Deltics' on menial passenger or parcels turns became predominant. Obviously, this under-employment could not continue, so the eight Haymarket and six Gateshead locomotives were re-allocated during March to York Depot, where it was hoped their sevices could be better utilized. York Depot men immediately took the 'Deltics' to their hearts, even to the lengths of acquiring permission to position the York City coat of arms on the cab sides. Now even the grubby ex-Gateshead members of the class started to look respectable, and the ex-Haymarket units were still kept in the condition to which they were accustomed. York's 'customization' of its 'Deltics' really started the ball rolling; further south at Finsbury Park Depot, 55003 *Meld* emerged on 6 April after being re-painted featuring white window surrounds, which from then on became the trademark of the surviving 'Deltics' at Finsbury Park.

Finsbury Park Depot as it will be best remembered, with three of its 'Deltic' allocation on view — left to right are 55009 Alycidon, *an unidentified Class '31', 55003* Meld *and 55012* Crepello (D. Carter Collection).

The next month, May, saw the beginning of the 1979/80 timetable, featuring the long-delayed inauguration of the East Coast's full Inter-City 125 operational timetable. Hot news to some, to the dedicated 'Deltic' enthusiast it was just an anti-climax, for on 14 May, just up the line from King's Cross, Finsbury Park Depot was at it again — polishing 55003 *Meld* until it glistened. The reason for this treatment was that the locomotive had been chosen to head a new high-speed service, the 'Hull Executive', from King's Cross to Hull on its inaugural down journey, departing from King's Cross at 17.05. What a sight *Meld* was, adorned with the suitably-inscribed headboard up front, and she departed on what was to be one of the all-time great runs for a 'Deltic'. The 138-mile non-stop section of its journey on this particular day was, unfortunately, interrupted by two dead stands, so Retford, its first diagrammed stop, was reached 14 mins late, but with a net time of 85 mins. The train's diagrammed time was actually 91 minutes, averaging 91.4 mph for the non-stop 138 mile run, so, with the two stops, *Meld* must have really been flying somewhere en route to achieve a net time of 85 mins. Even so late in their career, the 'Deltics' had been chosen to haul what was then the fastest locomotive-hauled train in Britain.

Unfortunately, the poor availability of these now aging machines was brought out into the daylight long before the 'Hull Executive' and its exploits, for earlier in the year, when the new timetable was being drawn up, the Chief Mechanical and Electrical Engineer predicted that only 50 per cent availability could be expected from the 'Deltics'. So, the new timetable was compiled using 'Deltics' on eleven diagrams, with only two daytime trains north of York. These were the 05.50 King's Cross to Aberdeen and the 10.43 Berwick to Plymouth, which later, after the opening of the Penmanshiel diversion, reverted to an Edinburgh departure but, as stated earlier, the 'Deltic' only worked as far south as York.

Now that York had settled down to the fact that it now had an abundance of 'Deltics', it certainly took no time in utilizing them. During May, 'Deltics' began to venture down the Scarborough line, where they had previously been largely unknown. No 55012 *Crepello*, although not a York locomotive, worked from Newcastle throughout to Scarborough on 7 May, even taking the trouble to run around its train at York. Apparently 55012 was used instead of the normally-rostered Class '40'. No 55013 *The Black Watch* was at Scarborough on 19 May heading a train for King's Cross, and was also seen heading a King's Cross train along this section on the 28th.

By June, the 'Deltics' had even begun to venture down the branch from Scarborough to Filey, where 55011 *The Royal Northumberland Fusiliers* was noted on 2 June. Later, 55011 set off towards Scarborough from Filey on the first leg of a Newcastle-bound train, which it worked as far as Scarborough only. It eventually departed from Scarborough on a through train from Bridlington to King's Cross.

Meanwhile, 'Deltic' activity continued on the Cleethorpes trains from London. Among a few instances of 'Deltics' being noted on this

55004 Queen's Own Highlander *at King's Cross resting between duties to the north* (D. Carter).

service during May was 55006 *The Fife and Forfar Yeomanry* on the 13.04 from King's Cross on both the 1st and 2nd, while the 5th saw 55007 *Pinza* on the same train. On the 6th, however, 55011 *The Royal Northumberland Fusiliers* was on the 11.05 from King's Cross, which set a precedent.

Since their move south, the 'Deltics' had by now become fairly rare in the Edinburgh area, apart from visits on the night sleepers and the daytime trains from London and Plymouth. However, four members of the class were noted in Edinburgh during May, so some 'Deltic' activity obviously remained, albeit on a small scale, such as on 7 May when 55022 *Royal Scots Grey* was used on the 16.45 Edinburgh-Aberdeen train with six Mk I coaches in tow.

By June, York Depot seemed to relish sending 'Deltics' to far-flung places, whether it be one of their own alloction or a London member of the class. This was exemplified on 19 June when 55015 *Tulyar* was a truly remarkable visitor to Liverpool, rolling into Lime Street on the 11.28 Newcastle-Liverpool train. This was the first occasion on which a 'Deltic' had been to Liverpool since the regular appearances of the prototype during the late 1950s. Then, on 5-6 July, 55013 *The Black Watch* was used throughout from the north-east to Liverpool and return. On the 5th 55013 had replaced Class '47' 47522 at York and had returned on the 19.05 from Lime Street; on the 6th it had been used on the 08.45 from York and the 13.05 return.

Nonetheless by June a large portion of the 'Deltic' fleet was in Doncaster Works. On 16 June seven units were present: 55001 *St Paddy* (which had been in the works since March 1978), 55020 *Nimbus* (which

55004 Queen's Own Highlander *being admired by a group of rail enthusiasts at Liverpool Lime Street whilst waiting to leave on a York-bound train* (D. Carter Collection).

had been there since April 1978 and which, during its stay, had become well-known for the pair of blackbirds which had the audacity to build their nest on it), 55002/4/8/15 and 16.

During the month, things looked a little brighter for 'Deltics' in the Edinburgh area, but not very much. On the 19th, both the Aberdeen sleeper and the 16.50 from Edinburgh to Aberdeen were 'Deltic'-hauled. On the 21st, the 08.50 Edinburgh to Aberdeen had 55018 *Ballymoss* at its head, which returned on the 12.40 from Aberdeen. Two days later the same diagram was worked by 55008 *The Green Howards*. The next month, on 25 July, *The Fife and Forfar Yeomanry* powered the 23.15 King's Cross to Aberdeen north of Edinburgh.

On Saturday 23 June an incident occurred which quickened the pulse of every 'Deltic' enthusiast in the north-east of England. The 05.50 King's Cross to Aberdeen arrived at Darlington double-headed by 55006 *The Fife and Forfar Yeomanry* piloting 55012 *Crepello*. On arrival 55006 was removed. I heard later that no stock had been available at Doncaster for the usual test train, so 55006 was quickly put on the 05.50

at Doncaster to be tested ahead of 55012. What 6,000 hp plus must have sounded like on the York to Darlington racing-ground that day is beyond the imagination!

A date that went down in the history of the East Coast Main Line was 20 August, for on that day the new route avoiding Penmanshiel Tunnel was completed and opened to rail traffic. So, the severed link was re-united and the East Coast route, for the first time, could really take advantage of its HST programme of InterCity 125 trains running at higher speeds than ever before between King's Cross and Edinburgh. One sad effect, of course, was the immediate withdrawal of the Edinburgh to Dunbar rail, then road-coach, connection service past the blockage to Berwick, which on quite a few occasions saw the use of 'Deltics'. Gone now was the sound and sight of a 'Deltic' tearing over Beattock on the diversionary route, racing its way up the Clyde Valley to Carlisle and Newcastle, except during very occasional future diversions due to engineering works.

Around August, the true availability of the 'Deltics' was difficult to calculate, with many locomotives undergoing maintenance and examinations at both York and Finsbury Park Depots. One thing, however, that was certain was that on 7 August nine 'Deltics' were in Doncaster Works — 55001/2/4/5/11/12/16/20 and 22 — the reason for the main hold-up at the works being apparently a shortage of power units. During a visit in the spring, one of these 'Deltics' (55016 *Gordon Highlander*) was standing outside in the open looking very forlorn. Externally it was extremely dirty, covered in oil stains on its lower regions and, having been in the works since 10 January, the weather had obviously taken its toll on the rest of its paintwork. The assistant's sliding cab window was broken and out of its runners, and one could only feel very sorry for 55016 in this sad state, but everything went well and, by October, 55016 was back in service.

In the meantime, 55015 *Tulyar* had followed 55003 *Meld*'s example by having its cab window surrounds and roof ends painted white by Finsbury Park Depot staff. *Tulyar* looked really splendid, and was exhibited at the Stratford Open Day. On Tuesday 31 July, BR Chairman Sir Peter Parker visited Finsbury Park Depot and was so impressed by the additions to *Tulyar*'s livery that, shortly after, permission was given for the whole Finsbury Park allocation to receive this treatment.

On 4 August, a 'Deltic' was unusually turned out to haul the 09.12 King's Cross to Skegness and the 13.35 return; the distinction went to 55006 *The Fife and Forfar Yeomanry*, and at that time it was only the second appearance of a 'Deltic' at Skegness. Another resort, Scarborough, was now a not uncommon host to 'Deltics', but on 26 July 55011 *The Royal Northumberland Fusiliers* arrived on a crew-training trip from York — a nice, easy and pleasant run out for 55011 and a change, no doubt, from the high-speed humdrum of the East Coast Main Line. The previous day, further north in Scotland, 55006 *The Fife and Forfar Yeomanry* was noted at Dundee on the 23.15 King's Cross to Aberdeen, so must have kept well after its test run the previous month with 55012.

55014 The Duke of Wellington's Regiment and 55004 Queen's Own Highlander await their next duties at King's Cross yard — perhaps, hopefully, as an HST stand-in...? (D. Carter Collection).

By September, the availability of the HST units had dropped to such a degree that it was not unknown for a 'Deltic' to stand in at a moment's notice. One such occasion was 13 September when 55019 *Royal Highland Fusilier* was turned out to deputize on no less a service than the up 'Flying Scotsman', composed of ten Mk I coaches, but no dining car. No 55019 put up a creditable performance, losing only 35 mins on this InterCity 125 service, which made one wonder yet again the practicality of building HSTs to gain, as in this case, only 35 mins over such a great distance and, at that, only to be utilized on the daytime services.

Towards October, the availability of the 'Deltics' took an upsurge and, by the second week of that month, only four Class 55s were in Doncaster Works. They were the two long-standing residents — 55001 *St Paddy* and 55020 *Nimbus* — together with 55004 *Queen's Own Highlander* which, after the fitting of two power units, was soon back in service, and 55018 *Ballymoss*, which was also soon back in service. All the Finsbury Park 'Deltics' were now running with white window surrounds — what a pity York did not follow suit with this very pleasing application instead of the normal drab all-over blue livery. However, York's allocation, with the exception of 55004, were sporting the now familiar York City coat of arms. Needless to say, upon release from Doncaster Works, 55004 soon joined them.

October was also a popular month for the 'Deltics' with rail-tour

Over 50 years of East Coast Main Line power line up at Carnforth during the 'Deltic' Preservation Society's railtour there on 14 October 1979 — 55009 Alycidon *lines up with* Sir Nigel Gresley *and* Flying Scotsman *(R. Newling-Goode).*

operators. On Sunday 7 October, T & N Railtours ran 'The Deltic Pioneer', hauled by 55022 *Royal Scots Grey*. The train ran from Manchester Victoria to Carlisle via Shap, then over to Newcastle and York, before returning to Manchester. The second tour was sponsored by the 'Deltic' Preservation Society, formed in 1977 with the aim of preserving a 'Deltic' in working order upon withdrawal. This train ran from York to Carnforth on Sunday 14 October and was named 'The Deltic Detour'. The locomotive chosen was an immaculate 55009 *Alycidon*. During the tour *Alycidon* became the first production 'Deltic' to enter a museum and was specially exhibited at 'Steamtown', Carnforth, alongside 'A3' 4472 *Flying Scotsman* and 'A4' 4498 *Sir Nigel Gresley*, a spectacle which resembled a line-up at a former Eastern Region shed, rather than this former ex-LMS stronghold!

To say that by the latter half of 1979 the 'Deltics' were beginning to fade in the realms of rail speed would definitely have been an overstatement. Although they had been robbed by the HSTs of their best chances to show their capabilities, they certainly began to excel themselves on the so-called semi-fast services. Despite this term, they were very tightly timed and, in the main, offered fairly short runs between stops, a type of service on which the 'Deltics' had previously been unknown. However, as usual, the class took to these trains like ducks to water, and gave everyone concerned a chance to sample the phenomenal 'Deltic' acceleration which was to rule these services.

The one exception to this new type of work for the 'Deltics' was the 'Hull Executive', which was scheduled to cover the 138.60 miles between King's Cross and Retford non-stop. To keep to the times this service demanded, the class, after any out-of-course delays, had frequently to exceed the 100 mph ceiling bestowed on them. It became known that speeds of 105 to 110 mph were being clocked with ease, and averages of 107 mph were quite frequently being logged for mile after mile — even Stoke Summit held no perils, with speeds of 102 mph being noted at the summit.

Even though these speeds could only be frowned upon by the authorities as a blatant breaking of regulations, it must be said, thank goodness, that there were still drivers around who were willing to have a go when time was lost. Many people have asked what the maximum speed of a 'Deltic' might have been on such a service train; without a doubt I can say that having studied many logs and talked to several drivers, one speed appears many times, that being 113 mph. Although I know that this speed has been surpassed, it seems that, under normal circumstances, this is the maximum for the class, but no doubt some will disagree.

The autumn of 1979 showed more 'Deltic' appearances on the Edinburgh to Aberdeen route. They were certainly still quite frequently sighted around Edinburgh where, for a time earlier in the year, enthusiasts had been saddened by the lack of them. Like the Cleethorpes trains, the Edinburgh to Aberdeen services only saw sporadic 'Deltic' haulage around this time, and not to any regular pattern. In fact, the mainstay of this Scottish service was still in the capable hands of the Class '40's, with a sprinkling of '47's.

One depot where 'Deltics' during their normal use would never be seen was Staveley, Barrow Hill, but this depot, along with others few and far between, held open days where the public and enthusiast alike could mix and inspect locomotives and stock at close quarters. The 1979 Open Day was held on 7 October, and York Depot obliged by sending 55016 *Gordon Highlander* as an exhibit, and it received a lot of attention from the crowds of people attending. It was in excellent condition, both internally and externally, having arrived at Staveley direct from Doncaster Works.

Now familiarized with the cross-Pennine route to Merseyside, the 'Deltics' during the latter half of the year showed no signs of making fewer forays into Midland territory. No 55017 *The Durham Light Infantry* was in Liverpool on 26 September with the 09.28 from Newcastle, while three days later 55012 *Crepello* arrived with the 08.45 from York and returned on the 13.05 from Liverpool. No 55002 *The King's Own Yorkshire Light Infantry* arrived in Liverpool on 10 October with the 08.14 from Newcastle, then on 27 October in came 55003 *Meld* on a train from Newcastle. The 20.40 train for York on 2 November was headed by 55019 *Royal Highland Fusilier*, while the next day 55003 *Meld* made another appearance on the 08.49 from York.

By the end of the year, therefore, BR had conceded by allowing the

York Depot 'Deltics' more, although not consistent, use over a wider area of the railway network, thus rendering them not quite as redundant as had been feared. In fact, their use on any class of passenger or parcels train had become so widespread that one never knew when to expect a 'Deltic'. On 3 November, for example, 55008 *The Green Howards* found itself heading a King's Cross to Middlesbrough football special. Meanwhile, further north in Scotland, the class was becoming more numerous in the Aberdeen area. On both 18 and 23 October, the 05.50 King's Cross to Aberdeen and the 16.30 Aberdeen to York were 'Deltic'-hauled. On 20 October the Scottish Railway Preservation Society ran a 'Deltic'-hauled special train from Falkirk to Aberdeen via the Perth to Dundee line, where the class was very rare indeed. Apparently, this was only the second occasion on which a 'Deltic' had traversed this stretch of line, the first being during January 1970.

The now more regular, but still inconsistent, visits of 'Deltics' to Aberdeen, Cleethorpes and Liverpool by late October had probably developed due to the commencement of the new timetable. This timetable left the class with only eleven scheduled diagrams, and with 55004 and 55016 back in service, and the higher availability of the 'Deltics' as a whole, it was not surprising, therefore, that these grand locomotives were utilized on other services which were diagrammed for, say, a Class '46' or '47' but where the superior power of a 'Deltic' was a definite help. Advantage was also taken when the 'Deltics' used on the overnight sleepers from the south had nothing to do during the daytime and were used on fill-in duties. This was most probably the reason for 55021 *Argyll and Sutherland Highlander* appearing on the 14.25 local from Edinburgh to Newcastle, and the sight of 55007 *Pinza* on 5 November

55007 Pinza *stands at Platform 1 at Darlington Bank Top on her way home from a foray in Scotland* (D. Carter).

near Shields Road, Glasgow, on a parcels train.

December arrived with Doncaster Works playing host to four 'Deltics' (55001 and 55020 were still heavily cannibalized, 55013 *The Black Watch* was in with a ruptured fuel tank and bodyside fire damage, while 55014 *The Duke of Wellington's Regiment* was receiving a light repair). Also, around this time 55009 *Alycidon*, 55012 *Crepello* and 55017 *The Durham Light Infantry* were restricted to electric heated stock only, which could only be due to boiler defects. Even so, the failure rate continued at a low level and showed more than the diagrammed eleven units available. This relatively optimistic state of affairs of course made it less likely that 55001 *St Paddy* and 55020 *Nimbus* would ever return to traffic again, especially during the last few months of 1979, when each day 13 or 14 'Deltics' were actually available for service.

Nonetheless, the official withdrawal date for the class was drawing nearer; the only ray of hope was that the shortage of motive power fitted with electric train heating equipment would continue, possibly giving the 'Deltics' a stay of execution. To conclude that 1979 was a year of regression for the class is fair, but in certain other areas it appeared to have also been a year of satisfaction.

1980

'...the withdrawal programme for 1980 stated that three 'Deltics' would fall victim...'

Satisfaction could hardly be the word to start off 1980, for during the week ending 5 January Eastern Region officially withdrew *St Paddy* and *Nimbus*. Dismantling of *Nimbus* began on the 8th and was completed on the 26th. Meanwhile, *St Paddy* was stripped of all usable parts and work began on cutting her up on 30 January.

Those two apart, by late January 'Deltics' present in Doncaster Works were: 55005 *The Prince of Wales's Own Regiment of Yorkshire*, suffering from a power unit defect; 55011 *The Royal Northumberland Fusiliers*, with fire damage; 55013 *The Black Watch*, in for an intermediate repair; 55014 *The Duke of Wellington's Regiment*, for one power unit to be

55001 St Paddy *awaiting the cutter's torch at Doncaster Works following withdrawal* (D. Carter Collection).

changed; and 55017 *The Durham Light Infantry*, with collision damage to number one end. (This damage was eventually repaired by removing the whole of the nose end from the top of the route indicator panel downwards. New sheet metal was then fabricated to form a new nose, utilising the hand rails, lamp brackets, tail lights, etc from the scrapped 55001 *St Paddy*. After completion of the repair, 55017 had the distinction of being the only 'Deltic' to run without a foot recess in one nose end above buffer beam height, and re-entered traffic in this guise on 28 March.)

The late January assessment of 'Deltic' availability definitely featured a downward trend and was not helped by the damage to 55011 and 55017. However, thankfully power unit failures were still low, so Doncaster's stocks were kept at a level whereby when 55014 visited the Works her stay was only short. In fact, she had previously remained in traffic for a while running on one engine only. During this spell she could obviously not be made available for top-class work, so York Depot utilized her on a strange assignment. On Friday 18 January, 55014 was despatched from York Depot en route to Crewe hauling locomotives destined for the works there, and actually entered the boundaries of Crewe Works with Class '47' 47305 and Class '40' 40147 in tow. Later it returned to York towing Class '46' 46049. On Tuesday 22 January, 55014 again left York, this time for Derby Works with Class '46' 46035 in tow. After this 55014 yet again returned to York, this time running light, before proceeding the next day to Doncaster Works to have her defective power unit exchanged. These travels had a happy ending when, on 25 January, 55014 was returned to traffic.

The early months of the year provided nothing conclusive as to the future of the class, with units making their usual sporadic appearances at Aberdeen and Cleethorpes, but they no longer appeared to dominate the York and Hull services. One highly unusual occurrence happened on the York-London service on 4 March when York Depot turned out 55013 *The Black Watch* and 55018 *Ballymoss* to work the up 12.15 to King's Cross. Meanwhile, on the Hull trains the 'Deltics' were still running well, particularly on the 'Hull Executive' service, a train on which they had really made their mark as regards speed and on which, time after time, they had never failed to excite the enthusiast.

May came and the class was still maintaining its fairly high availability, which came in very useful over the three-day Bank Holiday weekend from 3–5 May. Over this period, Eastern Region operated 127 extra trains, many of them utilizing spare 'Deltics'. Also over that weekend, on 5 May, Knottingley Depot held an open day and an obvious choice was for a 'Deltic' to be on show. York Depot obliged by sending 55002 *The King's Own Yorkshire Light Infantry*, which had actually been laid up at York since 20 April. Immediately after the open day, 55002 was returned to York for the continuation of repairs.

By 6 May, now that *St Paddy* and *Nimbus* had gone, there was only one 'Deltic' in Doncaster Works, 55019 *Royal Highland Fusilier*, which was undergoing an intermediate repair. It was also notable that during the March to May period, visits of the class to Liverpool had been few, possibly due to the improved availability of the Class '46's and '47's.

May also brought with it 'Rocket 150', the celebration of 150 years of the Liverpool & Manchester Railway and the Rainhill Trials. One feature of the festivities was a display of locomotives and rolling stock of the past, present and future displayed at Bold Colliery prior to the grand cavalcade at Rainhill. The organizers, besides wanting steam locomotives, also requested diesel and electric locomotives, both preserved and those still in service, so a 'Deltic' was, of course, a primary choice. (Personally, I have always thought that it was the decision to exhibit both diesel and electric locomotives which made 'Rocket 150' far superior to the Stockton & Darlington celebrations in 1975 when, with the exception of a Metropolitan Railway electric locomotive and the ungainly-looking prototype HST, the diesel age was ignored. Fancy holding an exhibition of railway history in the north-east of England, and committing the sin of not showing a 'Deltic'!)

The first choice of 'Deltic' for 'Rocket 150' was 55013 *The Black Watch*, which was chosen because it had recently received a re-paint which was further embellished by York Depot with features such as a silver-painted roof and fuel tanks, white wheel rims and buffer heads complete with white vacuum pipes etc. Quite a few 'Deltic' enthusiasts thought she looked rather incongruous but I thought she, at least, looked different and was a credit to the men of York Depot, who must have spent many hours of hard work on her. Under these circumstances, it seems unfair that in the end 55013 was chosen to be only the stand-by 'Deltic' for the exhibition, just in case the selected locomotive could not make it to Rainhill.

Another member of the class which at one time was thought to stand a chance was 55019 *Royal Highland Fusilier*; it had been in Doncaster Works undergoing an overhaul since 10 April and was expected to be available the week before the exhibition, but this did not materialize. The organizers then put a spoke in the wheel by requesting 55005 *The Prince of Wales's Own Regiment of Yorkshire,* which was to be sent to Stratford Depot for a re-paint and, no doubt, one of that depot's silver roofs but that also fell by the wayside.

The opportunity, perhaps not surprisingly, fell eventually to a Finsbury Park 'Deltic' to take pride of place (not that I am biased against the London 'Deltics' — one of them is my favourite), but after the work put in on 55013 at York I was lost for words, and I shudder to think what the men of York Depot thought! Anyway, as it happened, the final choice was 55015 *Tulyar*, on which Finsbury Park Depot must have lavished a great deal of time, for on the day she shone like a new pin and sounded in fine fettle. To reach Rainhill, *Tulyar* worked up to York to haul a train of vintage coaches from York throughout to Rainhill on

A glistening 55013 The Black Watch *in her Rainhill livery (as prepared by York Depot) about to depart on the 10.45 York to King's Cross train, 21 May 1980* (D. Carter).

21 May. What a picture this mixed-liveried train made traversing the trans-Pennine route!

At one point during the preparations at Bold Colliery sidings, *Tulyar* stood alongside the new West Coast Main Line's APT set 370004, and it was in this company that the 'Deltic' really did look dated. Also close by was the direct enemy, a production HST set, 253034. Other diesels present were Class '25' 25296, Class '45' 45068, Class '47' 47581 *Great Eastern*, the green-liveried Class '40' 40106, Class '56' 56077 and 08815. One very popular visitor was the maroon-liveried preserved Class '52' diesel-hydraulic D1062 *Western Courier*. Directly after the festivities, *Tulyar* was quickly returned to her old stamping-ground — the East Coast Main Line.

Without doubt, in their old age the 'Deltics' were being well looked after with regard to their external cleanliness, in some cases better than ever before, so it was most distasteful when an unforgivable incident occurred to 55018 *Ballymoss*. This incident came to light when, upon arrival at her home depot, it was discovered that someone had tried to remove one of her nameplates, badly damaging it in the process. The result was that for a short while *Ballymoss* was running in service minus one nameplate. Fortunately, the depot managed to straighten the plate without causing any more damage and so re-fit it in due course. This was the second instance of nameplate vandalism, the other member of the class involved being 55010 *The King's Own Scottish Borderer*, which did not come out of the trouble so well. The plate was so badly damaged that

55010 The King's Own Scottish Borderer *leaves Doncaster during 1980, without its nameplate* (D. Carter).

the locomotive ended its days running with only one. Also during the year some of the regimental-named members of the class were seen appearing without the crests above their nameplates, but whether these were removed illegally or not is not known.

Besides the Rainhill festivities, May brought with it the 1980 summer timetable, introduced on the 10th. Sadly, the 'Deltic' diagrams on this new timetable dropped to just ten per day. However, once this timetable had been in force for a while its effect on the class came to light. The 05.50 King's Cross to Aberdeen was 'Deltic'-hauled as far north as Edinburgh, and the class became more regular performers on the local trains between Edinburgh and Newcastle and vice versa. One particular anomoly was the 09.12 Dundee to King's Cross, the empty stock of which was 'Deltic'-hauled from Edinburgh at 06.40 to Dundee. It was then 'Deltic'-hauled throughout to London, but on several occasions this was not the case — either the train was Class '47'-hauled or the 'Deltic' just worked south from Edinburgh. One train which was almost predominantly 'Deltic'-hauled as far as York was the 09.50 Edinburgh-Plymouth, as was the corresponding down working in the afternoon. Apart from this, the class made good use of themselves on the overnight sleeper services and also on the York and Hull trains.

During the summer, due to the now better availability of the Class '47's, the 'Deltics' became more sporadic sights on the Cleethorpes trains, so leaving the class more readily available to work holiday extras. On a summer Saturday one did not know when to expect a 'Deltic'. At the northern end of the main line, they seemed to put in several appearances on extras from Scotland bound for Scarborough or Filey, which in previous years had only sported a Class '40'. The appearance of 'Deltics' at Scarborough was at its height on 5 July, when 55018 *Ballymoss* arrived at 07.10 light engine from York Depot, then later left for Filey with empty coaching stock to form a Filey-Newcastle train. At 09.10, *Ballymoss* re-appeared at Scarborough and waited at the buffer stops while 55008 *The Green Howards* attached itself to the other end of the train, departing for York and Newcastle at 09.25. When a path was cleared, *Ballymoss* drew out of the station and reversed on to the 09.54 departure for King's Cross, on which she duly worked south.

In fact, things were going so well that at the beginning of July there were no 'Deltics' in Doncaster works, but this was not to last, with 55015 *Tulyar* being laid up at Doncaster Carr Depot and close to shopping. However, it did reflect the good availability of the class at that time, even though 55007 *Pinza* was also in dock at Haymarket Depot with prolonged troubles, which were eventually to be rectified.

On 12 July, an unexpected 'Deltic' duo hit the East Coast Main Line, when 55009 *Alycidon* piloted 55008 *The Green Howards* into King's Cross on the 09.33 from Hull.

Another member of the class in trouble later that month, on the 25th, was 55016 *Gordon Highlander* on the 14.50 King's Cross to Leeds, deputizing for a failed HST. Apparently 55016 failed approaching Peterborough hauling a 9-coach train of Mk II stock. At Peterborough

North, Class '31' 31411 removed the expired 'Deltic' and took charge of the train for the remainder of its journey throughout to Leeds, where arrival was some two hours late.

From mid-July throughout August and September, availability of the class remained fairly high; although workings over foreign metals became fewer, visits to Cleethorpes remained frequent. One exception to a curtailment of the class's travels was on 7 September, when 55003 *Meld* made what was possibly the most unusual journey a 'Deltic' would ever make, being used to haul a special from Castleford in Yorkshire throughout to Blackpool North and return. In fact, *Meld*'s visit was only the second time a 'Deltic' had visited this popular resort, the first being the prototype 'Deltic' way back in the late 1950s.

A day earlier, the 6th, 55019 *Royal Highland Fusilier* was chosen to head a TBLS railtour from King's Cross to Edinburgh. This special was suitably named 'Cock O' The North', and 55019 bore a headboard suitably inscribed. I was at Ferryhill, Co Durham to witness 55019 pass by — and what a sight she was, nicely turned out and showing off the rather small but effective headboard! The special returned from Edinburgh at 17.30 headed by 55018 *Ballymoss* (a nice choice) and apparently made a rather exhilarating run with some very high speeds between Darlington and York.

The autumn arrived and with it the news that there were still more than the diagrammed number of 'Deltics' available, which meant that their availability was still high, with only three members of the class in Doncaster Works on 19 September. These were 55007 *Pinza* receiving a light repair after its long stay in Scotland; 55010 *The King's Own Scottish Borderer*, having an intermediate repair; and 55012 *Crepello*, undergoing

'Deltics' were always popular for railtours — 55018 Ballymoss *stands at Sheffield Midland on a tour from King's Cross to Doncaster and then to Tinsley Open Day, 15 July 1980 (D. Carter).*

repairs to its main generator.

Unfortunately, the next couple of months were to see a drop in availability, and by late October Doncaster was playing host to 'Deltics' 55002 *The King's Own Yorkshire Light Infantry*, undergoing an intermediate repair and an eventual re-paint to original two-tone green livery; 55012 *Crepello*, receiving rectification work; 55015 *Tulyar*, having power unit repairs; and 55019 *Royal Highland Fusilier*, awaiting return to traffic after receiving attention. Around this time, the white-capped London 'Deltics' were a rare sight, with only two units in service. Meanwhile, unusually, Aberdeen was playing host to 55008 *The Green Howards*, which was one of five active 'Deltics' north of Newcastle. The commencement of the winter timetable brought with it a change for the 10.05 from King's Cross, which from that time terminated at York, thence forming the 14.10 return to London, which became a 'Deltic' turn.

The September to November period began to show more sightings of 'Deltics' in the Liverpool area than in recent months; on 9 October, for example, 55004 *The Queen's Own Highlander* was utilized on the 08.49 York to Liverpool and the 13.05 return. During November, 55005 *The Prince of Wales's Own Regiment of Yorkshire* made three journeys to Liverpool. The first occasion was 4 November on the 08.49 to Liverpool and the 13.05 hrs return, while the second visit took place on the 11th, when 55005 was beautifully turned out by York Depot to haul a special to celebrate the 150th anniversary of 'Mail by Rail'. This special train had worked north from Liverpool earlier in the day hauled by one of the country's best preserved steam locomotives (No 46229 *Duchess of Hamilton*), so it was only fitting for this train to be taken back to Liverpool by the 'King of Diesels' — a 'Deltic'. Two days later, after returning to York, 55005 made its third return trip on 13 November. Other members of the class to reach Liverpool during this period were 55013 *The Black Watch* on two occasions; 55014 *The Duke of Wellington's Regiment* once; 55016 *Gordon Highlander* twice; 55017 *The Durham Light Infantry* twice; and 55022 *Royal Scots Grey*, which also made two return trips.

Towards the end of 1980, the 'Deltics' were making more trips on the Edinburgh to Aberdeen line and meanwhile, at the southern end of the main line, were still making their usual sporadic appearances on the Cleethorpes services. One 'Deltic' amongst others which spent a good while out of service during the autumn was 55003 *Meld*, but she did return to service for a while before troubles set in again.

November brought with it the sight of another 'Deltic' at Tees Depot, Thornaby, Cleveland. This time it was 55022 *Royal Scots Grey*, which arrived on 16 November for wheel-turning. This very large and modern depot, after being equipped with a large German-manufactured lathe, began to see all kinds of strange locomotives for wheel-turning, from small, privately owned diesels to many BR classes and HSTs, as well as preserved locomotives from the North York Moors Railway. No 55022 was, however, only the second 'Deltic' to receive treatment of this kind at Tees Depot, the first being 55005.

55022 Royal Scots Grey *awaits wheel-turning at Thornaby Depot on 16 November 1980* (D. Carter).

Possibly the greatest event to befall these almost twenty-year-old diesel locomotives happened inauspiciously on Friday 13 December when, after receiving a full intermediate overhaul at Doncaster Works and being re-painted in the original two-tone green livery, 55002 *The King's Own Yorkshire Light Infantry* entered the National Railway Museum at York for an official ceremony. This ceremony, heralded by a fanfare from soldiers of the Light Infantry, announced the news that 55002, upon withdrawal from regular BR service, was to become part of the National Collection, thus guaranteed to be preserved for all time. During the ceremony a plaque was unveiled on the locomotive's side to commemorate the occasion. It read 'This locomotive, to be preserved as part of the National Collection, has been repainted in its original colours, with a grant by the Friends of the National Railway Museum.' As soon as the festivities ended, 55002 was drawn out of the museum building by D2860, an ex-BR diesel shunter and itself part of the Collection at York. D2860 then drew clear to allow 55002 to start up its engines and move out of the museum boundaries. Once out on the main line, 55002 headed for York Station to haul the 14.10 York to King's Cross train.

By mid-December, although the withdrawal programme for 1980 had stated that three 'Deltics' would fall victim, it began to seem to the

55002 The King's Own
Yorkshire Light Infantry
after its National Railway Mu-
seum dedication ceremony, 13
December 1980 (D. Carter
Collection).

enthusiast as though this would never occur. For a long time it had been
rumoured that 55003 *Meld* was to be the next 'Deltic' to be withdrawn
and, although it had spent a certain amount of time out of service, it
always came back fighting (or so it seemed). The course of events for
Meld started on 14 November when she was returned to traffic from
Doncaster Works after receiving a power unit change. Once back in service *Meld* embarked upon the most precarious patch of her career, which
was to come to the inevitable, and the hardest and quickest, end of all.
On Christmas Eve, *Meld* was rostered to work a holiday relief train from
King's Cross to Edinburgh. At 15.03 she drew out of King's Cross and
disappeared into Gas Works Tunnel for the last time. All seemed well
until further north *Meld* began to suffer power unit and boiler problems
to such a degree that it was thought advisable to remove her from the
train at Newcastle. She was then quickly taken over to Gateshead
Depot, where she remained over the Christmas period, before leaving
light engine for York Depot on 27 December.

What it was hoped had been a successful repair at York was not, for
the sands of time were now set against *Meld*. On 29 December she
departed north from York on what was to be the last passenger train she
would ever pull, for by the time Thirsk was reached *Meld* was declared a
failure due to a coolant leakage and was returned light engine to York,

55003 Meld *leaving Gateshead Depot for withdrawal at York after limping from Thirsk to Newcastle on the down Plymouth to Edinburgh service, 29 December 1980* (D. Carter).

running on one engine only. The final decision to withdraw the locomotive was made on the afternoon of the 30th, with an official withdrawal date being set for the following day. Almost immediately, *Meld*'s traction motor blowers were removed for use in 55014 and one of her sliding cab windows was removed for 55002. Also at York Depot on that day was 55006 *The Fife and Forfar Yeomanry*, suffering from fire damage, so on the 31st *Meld* was attached to 55006 and the pair were towed away to Doncaster by Class '37' 37138.

Doncaster Works was closed for the Christmas and New Year period, so both 'Deltics' languished outside the boundary, within viewing distance of the station. *Meld* was eventually taken into the Works for the last time on 5 January 1981 to await the cutter's torch. Upon examination once inside the works, the verdict was one power unit pinned out due to constant coolant loss and the other unit also suspect; the boiler was non-operational.

It had been a mixed year for the 'Deltics' with the demise of *St Paddy* and *Nimbus* at the beginning, then the epics of the 'Hull Executive' to follow, only to end with the withdrawal of *Meld*. It was now only a matter of time before the axe was ready to strike again, but at least the 19 surviving locomotives had seen the end of another year.

1981

'...if a unit failed and required more attention than was considered viable... it would simply be withdrawn.'

The year had hardly begun when, on 5 January, timetable changes were introduced with a new service featuring an InterCity 125 service from Middlesbrough to King's Cross. It was hoped by enthusiasts in the north-east (and rumoured for a while) that this service was to be 'Deltic'-hauled, but alas this was not to be. If it had been, it may perhaps have caused a stay of execution for some 'Deltics', and it would certainly have brought the sight of a 'Deltic' or two each day at Tees Depot to break the monotony of the usual more mundane classes on view. Still, not only did this not happen, but worse — it was announced that from 5 January the 'Hull Executive' was to be turned over to HST operation. This really was a nail in the coffin for the 'Deltics', for what could possibly lie ahead for them now? There seemed very little to look forward to but a slow, lingering wait for the scrap-heap.

In fact, from the early part of the year it was understood that no more classified repairs were to be carried out on 'Deltics', which meant that if a unit failed and required more attention than was considered viable to repair, it would simply be withdrawn. This situation, therefore, could only mean that the exact order in which the class would be withdrawn would be very unpredictable.

The final demise of the 'Deltics' on the 'Hull Executive' denied them their last chance to show their true form and capabilities. This train departed at 07.00 from Hull and returned at 17.05 from King's Cross, its 'Deltic' adorned with the red-backed headboard, reflected the sight of the class in better days long gone. So it was on Friday 2 January when 55015 *Tulyar* departed from King's Cross with what was to be the last official trip for the 'Deltic'-hauled 'Hull Executive'. *Tulyar* was well-groomed for the occasion and, as well as the headboard, her nose end was adorned with a wreath to commemorate the occasion, this tribute being supplied by the Yorkshire branch of the 'Deltic' Preservation Society. Fortunately, as it turned out this was not to be the last 'Deltic'-hauled 'Hull Executive' for, although the last official train had run, BR decided to extend the use of both 'Deltics' and headboard on the equivalent weekend service to produce an extended 'last fling' on both the Saturday and Sunday. What a weekend that turned out to be — 'Deltic' enthusiasts came from far and wide to witness the events.

On Saturday, 3 January, the 07.00 southbound train departed behind the green-liveried 55002 *The King's Own Yorkshire Light Infantry* (a popular choice and a truly wonderful sight). Meanwhile, as 55002 journeyed south, at the London end all had not been forgotten, for ready at Finsbury Park Depot for the return 17.05 train was 55007 *Pinza*, specially turned out with red buffer beams, white buffer-heads etc — what a picture! Not only did *Pinza* make Saturday's down trip but also both of the final up and down trips on the Sunday, bringing the curtain down for the last time for the class on this service, and the end of an era. The next day, Monday 5 January, saw the inauguration of the HST reign on the Hull service.

Despite these events, the 'Deltics' made a reasonable start to 1981 with a fairly good availability rate. Apart from *Meld* lying dead in Doncaster Works, there was only one other member of the class in the works at the beginning of the year; as already mentioned earlier, this was 55006 *The Fife and Forfar Yeomanry* awaiting power unit repairs. Meanwhile over the border in Scotland, Haymarket Depot was playing host to 'Deltics' 55010/12/19 and 21.

The repairs to 55006 did not take long to complete and by mid-

Keeping the flag flying – 55017 The Durham Light Infantry *rolls into Durham on a down Plymouth to Edinburgh train* (D. Carter).

January she was back in service. I noted her at Darlington Bank Top Station on 23 January heading north on the northern leg of the Plymouth to Edinburgh train. On this occasion, 55006 looked well-used (that is, filthy) and, to add insult to injury, one of the sliding cab windows must have required repair, because someone had chalked on her cabside 'Keep shut', with an arrow pointing to the offending window. Although looking very dejected, 55006 was in fine fettle, for once clear of Bank Top she opened up and could be heard for quite a while powering away to the north. Unluckily, this good mechanical condition did not survive for long, for on 2 February, whilst hauling the 01.00 King's Cross to Newcastle, she suffered a power unit failure and was removed on arrival at York at around 04.40. No 55006 was then taken to York Depot where, on 3 February it was discovered that the fault had only been the minor one of the failure of the coolant flow switch. After replacement all seemed fine, but by then it was too late, for 'Deltic' 55006 was scheduled for withdrawal and was officially withdrawn on the following Sunday, 8 February.

That fateful day, 3 February, found 55005 *The Prince of Wales's Own Regiment of Yorkshire* present at York Depot undergoing a 'B' examination and suffering from a boiler defect so, being also scheduled for withdrawal, the decision was made to make her fate official on 8 February also. No 55005 eventually arrived at Doncaster Works on the 21st, and 55006 arrived on the 23rd. The latter was taken into the works' No 4 bay on 3 March and transferred from its existing bogies on to those removed from 37246, before being taken back out into the yard to await scrapping.

Dejected, forlorn, but not forgotton — the sad sight of 55005 The Prince of Wales's Own Regiment of Yorkshire *awaiting entry to Doncaster Works for the last time, 21 February 1981* (D. Carter).

The 'Deltic' Preservation Society's display at the National Railway Museum during 1981, commemorating 20 years of 'Deltic' service (D. Carter).

Better news later in the month was the 20th anniversary of the 'Deltics' in service on 28 February. This auspicious occasion was celebrated by 55022 *Royal Scots Grey* being rostered to work the 12.20 from King's Cross to York. Bearing a commemorative headboard supplied by the 'Deltic' Preservation Society, 55022 was the ideal choice for the occasion, being the second 'Deltic' to enter service (the first, 55001 *St Paddy*, had already been withdrawn). However, the event was almost marred earlier in the week when 55022 was declared a failure, but maintenance staff came to the rescue and got her into shape for the occasion. On the day *Royal Scots Grey* ran well, as was witnessed by the hundreds of fans who noted her passing, risking pneumonia in the typical British rain and snow! On arrival at York, the run was celebrated with champagne (provided by the 'Deltic' Preservation Society and enjoyed by driver George Craven along with other dignitaries), and afterwards 55022 retired to York Depot. David Carter, then 'Deltic' Preservation Society Chairman, presented Peter Semmens, Deputy Keeper of the National Railway Museum, with an engraved glass depicting 55022 (D9000) *Royal Scots Grey* to commemorate the opening in the Museum of the Society's own exhibition paying tribute to the twenty years' service of the 'Deltics'.

The following month, like February, was to be tinged with both grief and joy. On 12-13 March, the remaining nose sections of 55001 and 55020 were cut up, while 55003 *Meld* stood in Doncaster Works over at the 'Goliath' crane ready for stripping. In fact 55003 had been in the hands of the scrap-man since 9 March, and cutting up had begun; by the 11th both cabs had been removed and stood together. The bodysides remained to be cut up, leaving the frames and bogies to be taken care of.

By March it had become well known that Doncaster Works had stopped giving classified repairs to the 'Deltics', but, worse still, it was announced that even unclassified repairs were to stop. Power unit changes were excluded at this time but general overhauls on power units ceased. The last 'Deltic' to receive a general overhauled power unit was 55018 *Ballymoss,* which returned to traffic in this condition on 8 May. Even so, although general overhauled power units were now no longer available, some work on power units did continue on a modest scale while spare parts were still available, and power unit changes could

55015 Tulyar *stands outside Finsbury Park Depot on 17 March 1981 following the unveiling of plaques to commemorate her attendance at the Rainhill 'Rocket 150' celebrations* (R. Newling-Goode).

still take place, but for how much longer was then anybody's guess. The last member of the class to receive an unclassified repair was 55004 *Queen's Own Highlander,* which entered the works on 16 March and, besides various mechanical repairs, received attention for collision damage, a bent nose section. No 55004 was soon back to traffic on 19 March.

Meanwhile at Finsbury Park Depot during March, 55015 *Tulyar* had been fitted with two commemorative plaques on her nose ends to acknowledge her attendance at the 'Rocket 150' celebrations. These plaques, donated by the 'Deltic' Preservation Society, were unveiled at a ceremony held at Finsbury Park on 17 March in the company of the then 'Deltic' Preservation Society Chairman, David Carter, the Depot Engineer and the Society's Vice President at the time, Allan C. Baker. Upon *Tulyar's* withdrawal from service, it was understood that these plaques would be returned to the Preservation Society.

During this early part of 1981, the 'Deltics', although now dwindling in number, were still battling on, finding work when and where they could. Besides their more normal scheduled duties, they still appeared at Liverpool quite regularly and had even deputized for Class '47/7's on the Edinburgh to Glasgow InterCity trains; this duty fell to 55012 *Crepello* on 3 March although it seems impossible that a 'Deltic' would attempt to push such a train, not being fitted for push/pull operation.

On other occasions a 'Deltic' standing idle was a 'Deltic' to be used. For example, on 13 March 55011 *The Royal Northumberland Fusiliers* was standing at Peterborough between duties when it was quickly summoned to stand in for a failed DMU and was utilized on the 07.21 Peterborough to Spalding and the 07.56 return. Another day when spare 'Deltics' were made available was 4 April, for a special train from Huddersfield to King's Cross. No 55010 *The King's Own Scottish Borderer* worked the train to London and 55009 *Alycidon* was made available for the return working (not a bad record for a now doomed class of twenty-year-old, high-speed locomotives, chosen for such duties in preference to their more modern counterparts!)

During the spring, the 'Deltics' really began to sing their swan-song, being ever more sought after for use on specials. One such train ran on 25 April, chartered by the 'Deltic' Preservation Society and entitled 'The North Briton', from York to Edinburgh via Skipton, Carlisle and Carstairs, returning by way of the East Coast Main Line from Edinburgh to Newcastle, then using the coast route via Sunderland and Hartlepool, to regain the main line at Northallerton. On the morning of the 25th, the empty stock to be used on the excursion arrived at York from Leeds behind 55008 *The Green Howards.* Upon arrival at York, 55008 was uncoupled from one end of the train, while 55002 *The King's Own Yorkshire Light Infantry* was coupled up to the other end.

At 09.37, 'Deltic' '2' departed into a dark, wet, windy morning. All went well until a signal stop at Settle Junction, when the train drew forward on to the Carnforth line, which was not the planned route. The reason for this was bad weather further north, high up on the Pennines, with snow drifts blocking the line, so 55002 had to be re-routed via Carnforth and Shap. Once away from Carnforth, 'Deltic' '2' showed what a Class '55' could do with ten full coaches and, after 32 miles of almost unbroken climbing, passed Shap Summit at 58 mph, touching 96 mph on the descent to Carlisle. After departure from Carlisle, 55002 made an excellent run to the foot of Beattock Bank, passing this point at 87 mph, and after 10 miles of gradients averaging 1 in 75 speed only dropped to 56 mph at the summit. Once over Beattock the run featured a typical 'Deltic' descent to Carstairs, after which a more sedate run ensued to Edinburgh. The return journey by the more conventional route was taken with usual 'Deltic' ease, 55002 proving to be the master of its task, and after a round trip of 473 miles was back at York none the worse for its labours.

Just over a week later, 55002 was back again, heading another special on 4 May, 'The Deltic Fenman'. This train ran from London via Stratford, Bishops Stortford, Cambridge, Ely and March to reach Spalding, where it ran round its train to proceed through Peterborough to arrive at its destination — the Nene Valley Railway at Wansford. That day 55002 notched up a few 'firsts' for its class, being the first 'Deltic' to run on a preserved railway, the first to haul preserved (continental) coaching stock on a preserved line and the first to work between Fletton Junction and Orton Mere. 'Deltic' '2' was an amazing sight hauling *wagon-lits* and Danish State Railways stock on the 15.35 Wansford to Orton Mere. This tour proved to be such a success that a re-run tour was organized and took place on 25 May, this time featuring 55009 *Alycidon*. As usual, Finsbury Park did a marvellous job on cleaning up 'Deltic' '9' until she shone.

During May, it was not only on specials that the 'Deltics' drew attention to themselves. The 23rd saw an unusual incident when 55010 *The King's Own Scottish Borderer* failed at York, Dringhouses, with a broken air-pipe whilst hauling the 08.49 York to Liverpool. No 55011 *The Royal Northumberland Fusiliers* was quickly summoned and piloted 55010 plus train to Leeds, where both locomotives were replaced. Earlier in the month, on the 16th, 55016 *Gordon Highlander* was present in Doncaster Works suffering from a ruptured fuel tank. Fortunately, a spare tank was acquired, compliments of *Meld* (by then cut up). The availability of the 'Deltics' during the last week in May was very good; there was none in Doncaster Works at all, except for the withdrawn 55005 and 55006.

Continuing into June, Doncaster Works saw 55019 *Royal Highland Fusilier* arriving on the 9th for engine cylinder repairs, but was released back to traffic after only a few days. The only other member of the class to make a visit during June was 55021 *Argyll and Sutherland Highlander,* also for engine repairs. One other incident of interest in the Doncaster area was on 1 June, when 55017 *The Durham Light Infantry* was noted passing through heading north, running on one engine, towing dead Class '46' 46027 bound for York.

An item of news tinged with sadness was that as from 1 June

Finsbury Park Depot during 1981 with 'Deltics' 55008 The Green Howards, *55010* The King's Own Scottish Borderer *and, behind, a white-cabbed 55018* Ballymoss (T. Bye).

Finsbury Park Depot was to cease operations and all its locomotives were to be transferred elsewhere. The obvious and only choice for a new home for the depot's 'Deltics' was York, and it was a real pity that the depot's remaining 'racehorses' could not have run out their last few months from Finsbury Park. This depot had certainly given its Class '55's a touch of individuality during their last years and it was well-known that Finsbury Park staff just did not like to think of their 'Deltics' being allocated to another depot bearing their 'white cab' trademark. Thus these white painted surrounds over both cabs were removed before each 'racehorse' departed for its new home. In fact, such was the pride Finsbury Park had in their 'Deltics' that on 31 May 55009 *Alycidon* was specially turned out to work the 16.05 King's Cross to York, complete with commemorative headboard proclaiming 'Farewell Finsbury Park', and also bearing a wreath on its off-side lamp bracket. Also on board 55009 was Allan C. Baker, the Finsbury Park Depot Manager. *Alycidon* later returned south on the 19.10 York to King's Cross, and another era in the life of the 'Deltics' had come to an end.

No 55012 *Crepello* was at York Depot during early June, and had for a long time been rumoured to be due for withdrawal. The story of *Crepello*'s demise really began on 11 April when she left York with Class '37' 37194 in tow, bound for Doncaster, Hexthorpe Bridge. After a two-day sojourn, both locomotives entered Doncaster Works on the 13th. The fear was that this was the end for 'Deltic' '12', but not so. Once inside the workshops, number 1 power unit was dephased and changed; work was also carried out on the engine governors. By 17 April, *Crepello* was on test and was reinstated into traffic on the 24th. Alas, its life was to be short, for on Monday 18 May whilst undergoing a 'C' examination at Finsbury Park Depot, the decision was taken to withdraw the locomotive from service.

Finsbury Park staff removed some components before Class '31'

55018 Ballymoss *arrives at York from King's Cross shortly after transfer to York Depot. (Note that the white cab roof has been painted out)* (H. Watson).

31292 towed *Crepello* away for the last time, with *Alycidon* and *Tulyar* looking on. On 20 May, 55012 was en route to York Depot as a source of spare parts, and by early June had made its final journey to Doncaster Works, being towed there by 55014 *The Duke of Wellington's Regiment,* itself not in the best of health. Once inside the works, *Crepello* stood in the yard until 14 August, when her fuel tanks were removed, and by the 18th she was on the scrap line. On 2 September, 'Deltic' '12' was positioned at the 'Goliath' crane for final stripping, and by the 8th had lost both cabs; the following day her boiler was removed and one nose end cut up. The bodyside windows were removed on the 11th, and by the 14th one of her bodysides was in the process of being cut up. When the 16th came, only the sole-bar and water tanks remained — 55012 *Crepello* was now only a memory. As a postscript, a few months later a certain buffer arrived at Thornaby, Tees Depot, for a Class '37' which was thought to be from *Crepello* due to certain markings, so parts of her may still be in use somewhere.

However while one 'Deltic' was sinking into oblivion another member of the class was spreading its wings to hitherto unknown places and, for a now almost condemned class, for the most unusual reasons. One unusual occasion was 6 June when the green-liveried 55002 *The King's Own Yorkshire Light Infantry* was invited to attend Crewe Works Open Day, a grand gesture on the part of the London Midland authorities to a class of diesel locomotives which had competed against their electrics for so many years. No 55002 was specially cleaned for the occasion by York Depot, after arriving in that city from Edinburgh on 4 June. She left light-engine to Crewe on the morning of the 5th.

During June and July, the coast route through Stockton-on-Tees saw considerable use on various Sundays by diverted East Coast Main Line expresses, due to engineering works on the main line north of Darlington. This brought the last opportunity to see 'Deltics' on this route in any regular pattern. Living locally, I well remember hearing a 'Deltic' droning away in the vicinity of Stockton Station, then storming away to the south, being audible until it must have been leaving the outermost

55006 The Fife and Forfar
Yeomanry *departs from*
Darlington Bank Top on the up
Edinburgh to Plymouth service
(D. Carter).

boundaries of the town. The only Sunday I managed to visit the lineside
was 12 July, when 55016 *Gordon Highlander* and 55019 *Royal Highland*
Fusilier were noted in the space of a couple of hours.

There was now an increasing lack of 'Deltic' usage on the up and
down Edinburgh-Plymouth services. If the southbound service was
more than 10 mins late at Darlington, it could be almost taken for
granted that a 'Deltic' was not on the train. One such occasion was 21
July, when Class '47' 47509 *Albion* rolled in some 20 mins late on this
train.

During July, Doncaster Works undertook quite a lot of work on the
'Deltics'. On 16 July, 55005 was taken into No 2 bay for power unit
removal before being put back outside in the works' yard on the 17th.
No 55006 *The Fife and Forfar Yeomanry,* also withdrawn, remained outside
in the works' yard during the early part of July, complete with two
engines, but a decision was finally taken on 6 July to remove these for
use in 55009 *Alycidon* and 55022 *Royal Scots Grey.* At the same time,
'Deltic' '6' lost her fuel tanks and, after being drained, was positioned in
the yard ready for scrap; actual cutting up began on 8 July and by the
19th nothing remained.

Also in the works at the beginning of July was 55011 *The Royal Nor-*
thumberland Fusiliers, which received a bogie from 55012 *Crepello.* No
55011 had recently visited Tees Depot, Thornaby, for tyre-turning on
this suspect bogie, but the tyres were found to be undersize, so the
replacement bogie from *Crepello* was something of a godsend. 'Deltic'
'11' was back to traffic on 3 July. On the 8th, 55013 *The Black Watch* was
in the works for a power unit change, after suffering auxiliary drive
defects, but was back in service on the night of 15 July. On that day
55014 *The Duke of Wellington's Regiment* entered the works for an engine
change, which was done so quickly that the locomotive was ready for
traffic later that same evening. Another 'Deltic' also to undergo an
engine change during July was 55022 *Royal Scots Grey* on the 6th; a
coolant leak was getting into the engine sump. No 55022 was back in
service by the 10th. No 55021 *Argyll and Sutherland Highlander,* after

receiving quite a large amount of attention including a power unit change during June, was back in the works on 14 July for another engine change. This engine was effectively installed, allowing 'Deltic' '21' back into traffic on the 16th.

Although now well into their last summer, the 'Deltics' still continued to spread their field of activity on normal service trains, not only on the Carlisle to Edinburgh services, but also making appearances at the head of the 16.30 Aberdeen to Leeds. In fact, 'Deltic' activity in the Aberdeen area around that time had reached the stage where at least one member of the class was to be seen almost every day, possibly due to an overnight abundance of 'Deltics' at Haymarket Depot.

In August, British Rail decided to use 'Deltic's on two planned excursions from Edinburgh to Oban and return. The dates set were the 6th and 23rd, utilizing 55021 *Argyll and Sutherland Highlander* on both occasions, coupled to a strengthened set of Mk III coaches from the Glasgow-Edinburgh push/pull service. Both of these special trains were unique among the final few 'Deltic' excursions in that neither was advertised in the press or on stations as being booked for Class '55' haulage. They were both known simply as 'Festival Express' tours. The reason for this was that it was not decided by British Rail to use a 'Deltic' until the Thursday before the first tour ran, and this came about only because of the use of Mk III coaches instead of an 8-coach train of Mk I stock. The change of stock meant that the usual Class '37's on the Oban line would be of no use because they were not fitted with electric train heating equipment. The next choice of power might have been a Class '47', but they are not allowed on the West Highland line because of their heavy axle load, so the only suitable class available for both stock and road was a 'Deltic'. On both excursions, 55021 *Argyll and Sutherland Highlander* behaved admirably, the first and last 'Deltic' ever to traverse the Oban line. On the train itself things were particularly strange due to the absence of large numbers of rail enthusiasts but, even so, many photographs of these two memorable occasions still reached the press.

During August, the future National Collection showpiece, 55002 *The King's Own Yorkshire Light Infantry,* suffered some defects and was in Doncaster Works on 12 August for No 2 power unit to be changed. This replacement was completed and tested, and 'Deltic' '2' was ready for traffic by the 18th. After only two days' freedom, however, 55002 was back in the works with its No 2 end drive shaft sheared and a disintegrated flexible coupling from the gearbox. On the 27th, the locomotive was in Doncaster No 2 bay and during the night shift had an engine change. All repairs now completed, 55002 was released to traffic on 28 August.

Earlier in the month, 55002 had put in an appearance at Whitby on Sunday 2 August. This was the first time that a 'Deltic' had traversed this North Yorkshire branch from Middlesbrough via Battersby and Grosmont. The occasion was a one-day BR special return excursion from Newcastle via the coast route through Sunderland and Hartlepool. This tour was repeated on 30 August and was again scheduled for *The*

55002 The King's Own Yorkshire Light Infantry *arrives at Stockton-on-Tees returning from Whitby to Newcastle on 2 August 1981 and being admired by the author and his son Craig on the platform* (B.R. Macaulay).

King's Own Yorkshire Light Infantry, but this seemed impossible due to its temporary sojourn in Doncaster Works. All the local enthusiasts hoped that another Class '55' would be used, but of course, this was not necessary as 55002 was released into traffic two days before the train ran.

Although 'Deltic' performance during the high summer of 1981 did not take an adverse turn, it was becoming obvious that the class was making more frequent visits to the works than previously. Once the summer had passed, it was to be only a matter of time before more of them would be withdrawn.

The final run-down

*'...neglect, which is always associated with a
doomed class, had taken its toll...'*

The autumn of 1981 brought with it the final run-down of the 'Deltics',
and they entered the history books of the railways of Britain in a way
quite unlike that of any other class of diesel or steam locomotive. The
Class '52' 'Western' diesel-hydraulics went out in great style, but I do
not think anything could compete with the way in which the remaining
'Deltics' were sought after by enthusiasts, each one being photographed
or tape-recorded every time it was used.

It was on special railtours that the 'Deltics', after the end of August,
were to make their mark, travelling over routes upon which the class had
never before ventured. Even British Rail realized the potential in
revenue to be earned utilizing 'Deltic'-hauled trains. One such tour ran
on Saturday 12 September and was entitled 'The Deltic Anglian'; it ran
to the Nene Valley Railway and sported a headboard fixed to the chosen
locomotive No 55007. *Pinza* looked magnificent as she stood in Finsbury
Park Station that morning with her silver buffers, red beams and white-
rimmed wheels. The route chosen was Finsbury Park to Stratford, then
up the ex-Great Eastern main line to Ipswich for a crew change. The
next port of call was a photographic stop at Bury St Edmunds, after
which the train passed Ely and March before coming to a halt at
Spalding, where *Pinza* ran round the train.

From Spalding it was not long before Peterborough was reached,
and here *Pinza* picked up a pilot–man to instruct the driver over the Fletton Junction to Orton Mere line, over which there was a 10 mph speed
restriction. After arrival at Orton Mere, Nene Valley Railway, a very
vain-looking *Pinza* stood whilst hundreds of enthusiasts took her picture,
while between Orton Mere and Wansford 'Deltic' '7' must have been
photographed many thousands of times! Upon arrival at Wansford, *Pinza* received a rather pampered though well-earned rest until 17.20, when
it was on its way back to Peterborough. At Peterborough, 55007 ran
round the train once again, before heading off back to London via the
class's hallowed racing-ground, the East Coast Main Line.

A month earlier, on 15 August, 55007 *Pinza* had been an unexpected visitor to Liverpool Lime Street. Apparently, after receiving certain attention at York Depot, it was decided to try her out on the 15.40 from York and the 21.15 from Liverpool return. The occasion was highlighted by the fact that, apart from the withdrawn *St Paddy* and *Nimbus, Pinza* was the last of the surviving 'Deltics' to reach Liverpool.

Saturday 19 September was the last day for many of the summer-only East Coast Main Line trains which had utilized Class '55' haulage during this last summer of 'Deltics' in BR service, so it was nice to see a well-groomed *Pinza* at the head of the 09.45 Scarborough to King's Cross, leaving York in fine style for the journey south.

Besides travelling over strange routes on specials, the Class '55's were now in demand at depot open days. One of the most unusual callings was on 20 September, when Old Oak Common Depot, Western Region, was celebrating its 75th anniversary. That Sunday almost 20,000 people passed through the depot to view the exhibits, which included 55014 *The Duke of Wellington's Regiment.* 'Deltic' '14' had been specially cleaned for the occasion and was housed in Old Oak's heavy maintenance shop. What a sight she looked stood alongside Class '50' 50039 *Implacable* and Class '47' 47513 *Severn!*

When the 1981 summer timetable came to an end along with its extra trains, it was to be expected that more 'Deltics' would be made redundant. Under these circumstances it was not long before the axe fell upon 55018 *Ballymoss* on Monday 12 October. On that fateful day, it was noted on arrival at King's Cross that *Ballymoss* had sustained a power unit defect whilst hauling an overnight sleeper from Scotland. Unfortunately for 'Deltic' '18', the last three remaining spare power units at Doncaster Works had just been allocated, so the decision was quickly made to condemn the locomotive. So it was that *Ballymoss* returned north from London on one engine heading the 19.40 King's Cross to Hull; on arrival at Doncaster it was removed and ran light engine to York Depot for partial cannibalization. Useful parts removed, *Ballymoss* was towed south for Stratford Depot in north-east London, on its way being deposited for the last time at Finsbury Park Depot. In the company of condemned Class '40' 40068, *Ballymoss* finally made its way to Stratford for further stripping. Once there 55018's good engine was removed and transplanted into a willing *Pinza.* Eventually *Ballymoss* was towed to Doncaster Works, where cutting up commenced on 12 January, 1982.

The next 'Deltic' to be withdrawn was 55004 *Queen's Own Highlander,* which had two years previously escaped from Doncaster Works after being very close to condemnation. The unique aspect of the withdrawal of this 'Deltic' was that it was announced while the locomotive was away from the Eastern Region working the 15.50 York to Liverpool train, on one engine only. Upon arrival at Liverpool Lime Street Station, it was declared a failure. Rumour has it that the driver of sister locomotive 55011, also on Merseyside that day, was asked if he would haul his own train plus 55004 back to York, but he refused. So it was that the evening of 28 October saw a rather dejected 55004 awaiting

In happier times — 55018 Ballymoss at York, 24 February 1981 (D. Carter).

a tow back home to York, which came the next day courtesy of Class '31' 31405. The path set for the two was to follow behind the 13.05 Liverpool to York, hauled by 55002. Once back at York, the usual stripping took place before 55004 was towed south to Stratford Depot on 29 October, along with Class '47's 47019 and 47411. Stratford did not take too long to utilize any worthwhile parts and on 23 November 55004 was on its way back to York being towed in the company of 55011 and 55018. Back at York for the last time, it was only a matter of time before *Queen's Own Highlander* was taken to Doncaster Works for cutting up.

Withdrawal for 55011 *The Royal Northumberland Fusiliers* came on 8 November after a power unit failure. 55011's last year in service had been quite eventful; it acquired the art of occasionally catching fire, but luckily on each occasion never sustained enough damage to warrant withdrawal. In fact, 'Deltic' '11' had a charmed last few months indeed. After being sent to Thornaby Depot for tyre-turning, it was discovered that the tyres on one bogie were so worn that they could not withstand any more turning, but as luck had it 55011 was taken to Doncaster Works and underwent a bogie exchange with the withdrawn *Crepello*. However 55011's luck did eventually run out, and at Stratford Depot her good engine was fitted into 55008 *The Green Howards*. Useful parts removed, 55011, as previously mentioned, joined 55004 and 55018 for the long tow back to York Depot on 23 November. The following day,

Not long before withdrawal, 55011 The Royal Northumberland Fusiliers comes to a stop at Doncaster on the 05.50 King's Cross to Aberdeen (D. Carter).

both 55011 and 55018 were in Doncaster Works to await their fates.

November was to mark the end of an era at Doncaster Works when the last 'Deltic' engine to be completely overhauled was fitted into 55017 *The Durham Light Infantry*. The occasion was celebrated on Monday 16 November when 55017 was pushed out of the works' No 4 bay at the Crimpsall Shops. A television camera crew were present to film the event, including the breaking of a bottle of champagne over the locomotive's front end. In a strange way a good time was had by all, but behind the scenes there was an unmistakable air of sadness over the event, for this was now really the end of the excellent job carried out by the men of Doncaster Works.

At this point, it should be mentioned that once Doncaster had finished 'Deltic' power unit overhauls etc, it was the men of Stratford Depot, London, who became responsible for such tasks as engine and bogie changes, along with other numerous jobs, so special thanks should go to those men whose efforts kept the remaining '55's soldiering on to the end. Along with this, the very highest honours must go to York and Finsbury Park Depots for their undying labours with these magnificent machines, albeit such awkward beasts on which to work. Most of all, who will ever forget York's turnout of 55013 *The Black Watch* as the Rainhill stand-by, and Finsbury Park's wonderful efforts on 55015 *Tulyar*, the 'Deltic' actually used there?

York men really did love those machines and I will never forget my visit to York Depot on 31 October 1981 when, after walking around the shed yard and noting 'Deltics' 55008, 55010 and 55017 (which had, the day before, just returned from tyre-turning at Thornaby), I could hardly believe my eyes when, inside the shed itself, stood 55015 *Tulyar,* 55009 *Alycidon* and 55022 *Royal Scots Grey,* all fresh in a new coat of paint and, along with 55002 *The King's Own Yorkshire Light Infantry,* chosen to haul the farewell 'Deltic' specials. No 55022 actually emerged to work out its last days boasting its original number D9000 on both bodysides, at one end only. Once outside again, I was just in time to witness the passing of 55002 working 'The Celtic Deltic' rail tour en-route to Scotland. The day culminated in an opportunity to speak to drivers Arundale and Taylor, both top 'Deltic' drivers (along with Harry Wilson, who was not there that day). These men were not only drivers of the highest order, but real 'Deltic' enthusiasts of a very friendly nature — true ambassadors for British Rail.

Earlier in October, there was scheduled on the 17th perhaps the most unusual of the final excursions, 'The Wessex Deltic'. This train was scheduled to run across London from Finsbury Park to join the old London & South Western main line to Bournemouth for an Eastleigh Depot Open Day. The locomotive chosen for this tour was 55015 *Tulyar,* and for the occasion had been reunited with white cab surrounds, showing all those Southern Region diesel enthusiasts what a *real* diesel looks and sounds like! All went well with *Tulyar,* which no doubt enjoyed the different company of Class '33' diesels and Class '73' electro-diesels instead of the usual East Coast Main Line types. Once away from Eastleigh, 55015 made the return trip home via Fareham, Portsmouth and the cross-London link back to Finsbury Park.

The next tour to utilize a 'Deltic' was the 'Deltic Salute' on 24 October, and was to be the last excursion sponsored by the 'Deltic' Preservation Society during the class's life in everyday British Rail service. Motive power was to be yet again 55015 *Tulyar* for this run from York to Aberdeen and return, featuring photo stops at Dunbar, Dundee and Montrose. No 55015 departed from York at 09.30 on a typical English overcast, showery, autumn day. After stops to pick up at Darlington and Newcastle, 'Deltic' '15' sped on towards the first photo stop at Dunbar. Here, unfortunately, total irresponsibility took over when, to obtain photographs of *Tulyar,* certain people took it upon themselves to stand in the middle of the main line. Luckily nothing was coming, but this incident reflected badly on plans for forthcoming photo stops at Dunbar.

Once away from Dunbar, *Tulyar* settled down to a nice canter towards Edinburgh's Waverley Station, after which 55015 crossed both the Forth and Tay bridges, and made little effort navigating the at times arduous Fife coast line. Dundee was the next scheduled stop for photographs and *Tulyar's* boiler water tank was also topped up. Once away from Dundee, 55015 made good progress to the next photo stop at Montrose, before continuing on to Aberdeen. After arrival in the 'Granite City', 'Deltic' '15' ran light engine out to Ferryhill Depot for

55008 The Green Howards *arrives at York on the 10.05 from King's Cross* (D. Carter).

refuelling and a check-over. On the return, *Tulyar* got about a mile away from Aberdeen Station before coming to a stand due to a points failure; this cost 55015 about 40 mins in lost time, but once on the move, 'Deltic' '15' spared no pains in getting her train and all concerned back to Newcastle, Darlington and York.

It was not long before 55015 *Tulyar* was once again on its way to Scotland, this time at the head of another special entitled 'The Deltic

Queen of Scots' on 7 November. This tour ran from King's Cross to Edinburgh by a devious route, stopping at Peterborough, Grantham and Doncaster then deviating over to Leeds before regaining the main line before York. Northwards from York, *Tulyar* sped over the Great York Plain, before easing down for the turn-off on to the Tees line at Northallerton for the next stop at Hartlepool. After negotiating the Durham and Wearside coastal line, *Tulyar* arrived at Newcastle Central, then followed the East Coast Main Line to a photo stop at Dunbar, before finally reaching Edinburgh.

Unlike the previous tour, 55015 *Tulyar* was not rostered for the return back to London — instead, the immaculate green-liveried 55002 *The King's Own Yorkshire Light Infantry* was used. Once away from Edinburgh 55002 showed her prowess to her seated audience with a typical 'Deltic' performance heading south for Newcastle. Unlike the northbound run, once over the King Edward Bridge across the River Tyne, 55002 veered right to take the normal East Coast route through Durham and Darlington to reach York. Given the 'right away' from York, 'Deltic' '2' deviated over to Leeds, before making a good run to King's Cross via Doncaster and Peterborough. During almost the whole of this tour the weather was atrocious, with heavy mist, fog and rain.

One week later, on 14 November it was nice to see a different Class '55', this time 55009 *Alycidon,* at the head of a tour train called simply 'Deltic Cumbrian'. This tour originated at King's Cross and ran to Leeds, then over the picturesque ex-Midland Anglo-Scottish route to the north via Settle, and included a photo stop at Dent, which had probably not seen so many people since the final steam specials of the late 1960s. Once away from Dent, 55009 wasted no time in getting to Carlisle before returning to King's Cross through Hexham, Newcastle and the East Coast Main Line — good value for money at only £15.00 per head.

The 'Deltics' may have looked and sounded well at the head of their special tour trains, but behind the scenes, by mid-November, all was not well. By now, neglect, which is always associated with a doomed class, had taken its toll; with low priority for repairs and with spares not forthcoming, it was not long before 55002 and 55014 *The Duke of Wellington's Regiment* were stopped awaiting materials. 'Deltic' '2', being one of the chosen tour locomotives, was given priority and soon returned to service but, alas, 55014 never did, although, thankfully, it helped provide spares to keep the remaining 'Deltics' in service, together with 55004, 55011 and 55018. Following withdrawal on 22 November, due to its non-availability at York Depot, one of 55014's traction motors was transferred to one of the tour locomotives, possibly 55002. It seemed a trivial matter to have withdrawn 'Deltic' '14' on this score, but there was only just over a month to go before the whole class would be withdrawn from service, so it was obvious that the repair of 55014 would not have been a viable proposition. However, in its last few months 55014 did earn some distinctions for itself, the first being its previously-mentioned display at the Old Oak Common Open Day. The second was

The doomed 55014 The Duke of Wellington's Regiment *passes Bradbury on the up Edinburgh to Plymouth train* (H. Watson).

its use on 3 October to work the final 12.05 King's Cross to York. It was indeed to the credit of 'Deltic' '14' that, during her last few months in service, she had really put up some exceptional speeds whilst being stop-watched and timed over various sections of the East Coast Main Line, so boasting her personal popularity with 'Deltic' enthusiasts. It was truly a sad day when, on 24 November, 55002 towed 40058 and 55014 south to Stratford Depot, London. By early December, 55014 was back in the confines of Doncaster Works for the last time, awaiting breaking up.

The remaining running was now left in the hands of only twelve Class '55's — numbers 55002/7/8/9/10/13/15/16/17/19/21 and 22.

The end

'One man sank down on his knees and wept.'

To commemorate the demise of the 'Deltics' the final few tours of the class brought with them heart-felt emotions from both enthusiasts and railmen alike. Expense was no object to the 'Deltic' fraternity, who travelled hundreds of miles in some cases to see their favourite locomotive pass by into oblivion.

Two tours of special interest were 'The Deltic Venturer' and 'The Deltic Devonian' on 28 November 1981. Both of these tours involved taking two 'Deltics' over routes parts of which had previously been unknown to the class, and involved much planning by the authorities to make sure that crews were provided with the correct traction knowledge to handle a Class '55' so far away from home and over such strange ground. Under these circumstances, the driver was given the help of a 'pilot driver' who was familiar with the route concerned and who could give valuable advice regarding gradients, curves, speed restrictions and so on.

'The Deltic Devonian', sponsored by British Rail, had a nice surprise in store in that the rostered locomotive, 55002 *The King's Own Yorkshire Light Infantry*, was declared a failure on the morning of the tour, so a quick and suitable replacement was found in the form of 55016 *Gordon Highlander*, to almost everyone's delight. Bearing in mind that 55016 was not one of the final four specially-prepared 'Deltics', it did very well and did not let Eastern Region down. The train started from Finsbury Park Station and gained the Western Region via Canonbury Junction, Stratford, Temple Mills and South Tottenham, then the North London line to Acton Main Line Station to make a pick-up stop. Next port of call was Ealing Broadway for crew purposes, then 55016 was on its way to Exeter St Davids via the Berks & Hants line. The highlight of the section from Taunton to Exeter was the topping of Whiteball Summit at 75.5 mph, culminating in a one minute early arrival at Exeter. No 55016 actually ran the 164.40 miles from Southall to Exeter St Davids in 129 mins 14 secs at a start-to-stop average speed of 76.3 mph.

Once at Exeter, 'Deltic' '16' had a well-deserved one-hour rest

A sneaky shot over the wall at Doncaster Works of 55016 Gordon Highlander *standing behind the two-way road traffic mirror. Luckily 'Deltic' '16' after Works' attention, did receive an external clean before working the 'Deltic Devonian'* (H. Watson).

before attacking the 1 in 37 incline up to Exeter Central Station. This formidable bank was breasted at 23 mph and I doubt if a diesel locomotive, either before or ever again, will make as much fumes and noise as *Gordon Highlander* did that day! The return route to London was via the old London & South Western line to Clapham Junction, taking in a photo-stop at Salisbury. After leaving Clapham Junction, 55016 made its way back to the Eastern Region via the West London line to Willesden High Level and on to Stratford, thence to the unusual destination of Liverpool Street.

The other tour of the day, 'The Deltic Venturer', sponsored by the Severn Valley Railway, featured 55022 *Royal Scots Grey*, beautifully turned out by York Depot. No 55022 departed from York after the now traditional rapturous 'Deltic' send-off and took no time to reach Chaloners Whin Junction, there taking the Sheffield line. The start from Sheffield was 6.5 mins late, which *Royal Scots Grey* had almost made up by Clay Cross. However, just after Belper 55022 first suffered checks and then a stop for a vacuum problem in the brake system. This problem was to dog 'Deltic' '22' throughout the tour, accentuated by the use of old Mk I stock, which seemed to be in need of maintenance. Fast running commenced once clear of Derby and, although 55022 was 4 mins early into Birmingham New Street, the use of Mk I stock restricted speed to 90 mph which did not help matters on the faster stretches of this tour.

After a 7.5 mins late start from New Street, 'Deltic' '22' proceeded with caution until clear of the Lickey Incline. Once past Bromsgrove, 55022 decided to show what she could still do after twenty years' running, with a 90.5 mph average speed for the 25.50 miles between Stoke Works Junction and Cleeve, passing Cheltenham only 1 min.late. Once clear of Gloucester, *Royal Scots Grey* took to the Stroud line at Standish Junction and made light work of the 50 mph speed restriction on the climb up to Sapperton Tunnel. Once past Kemble, all looked well for an on-time arrival at Swindon, but due to platform occupation 'Deltic' '22' was checked, eventually arriving 1.5 mins late at Swindon's platform 3.

Away from Swindon, everyone thought sparks would fly but, yet again, because of the use of Mk I stock, 55022 was robbed of any chance of three-figure speeds and had to settle for a rather mundane trip into London, and, with out-of-course restrictions, 55022 did extremely well to reach Paddington only 6 mins late. Departure time from Paddington was 16.16, with a scheduled 50-min run to Oxford. However, after encountering severe delays at Reading and again at Didcot, a rather upset 55022 departed Oxford for Worcester 11.5 mins late after being refused certain glory on the high-speed Paddington to Didcot section. The Oxford to Worcester section also proved to be an obstacle to 'Deltic' '22' for, after numerous delays, arrival at Worcester was 16.5 mins late.

Clear of Worcester, *Royal Scots Grey* was now ready to show her capabilities to all with a magnificent climb of the Lickey Incline, hauling 11 coaches. The achievement was greater because of a 20 mph engineering slack at Bromsgrove, at the very foot of this famous incline. On the ensuing climb, 55022 accelerated from the 20 mph restriction to 30 mph at the summit, producing 2,430 edhp and developing 3,030 bhp at the crankshaft — a superb effort at such low speed for a predominantly high-speed machine used to the fairly gentle gradients of the East Coast Main Line. Once triumphantly over Lickey, 55022 took things easy with a comfortable run into Birmingham New Street Station. Departure thence was 19 mins late and, after the normal vociferous start, 'Deltic' '22', once past Kingsbury, held a steady 90 mph until power was eased for Burton-on-Trent. Between Burton and Derby this incredible locomotive did not let matters rest, for by Stenson Junction she had worked up to 92 mph before easing down for the customary slow approach to Derby.

Once away from Derby, *Royal Scots Grey* was now only 10 mins late and wasted no time in regaining more arrears, passing Chesterfield at 80 mph and powering through Sheepbridge at 73 mph at the beginning of a 4.75-mile, 1 in 100 ascent to Bradway Tunnel, which was entered at 62 mph. Still not giving up, 55022 flew through Millhouses, on the outskirts of Sheffield, at 75 mph, before arriving at Sheffield Midland Station only 1.5 mins late. Now shrouded in glory, 55022 departed from Sheffield, having attained many not-to-be-forgotten memories of itself for posterity, and, once back at York, after a very hard day's work, *Royal Scots Grey* retired to York Depot, a still more famous grand old lady.

December 1981 brought with it the ultimate realization that this was the last month of service for the remaining 'Deltics'. As each Class '55' went by, one wondered if it would ever be seen in service again and, of course, this eventually became a reality. The encroachment of HSTs not only on the East Coast Main Line but also on the North-East to South-West route, brought with it sheer boredom for many dedicated 'Deltic' enthusiasts, and others. In fact, by late 1982 matters had got so bad that it even became a treat to see a Class '47'-hauled passenger train

55008 The Green Howards rests at York Depot shrouded in glory a few days after a nocturnal 120 mph plus burst down Stoke Bank behind a nameless, very kind, York driver, 31 October 1981 (H. Watson).

during my still frequent visits to Darlington.

During their final few weeks, the class seemed to be enjoying a lot of nocturnal activity, mainly during the first half of December. On 10 December, of the survivors only 55021 *Argyll and Sutherland Highlander* was detained at York Depot for repairs, which were soon carried out, before resuming service. However, a week later matters had considerably altered, due to different circumstances. No 55015 *Tulyar* suffered a small fire while in Scotland and, after a few days on Haymarket Depot, Edinburgh, returned south to York light engine, thankfully fit enough to carry on. Also by then, 55010/13/19 and 21 were all running on one engine only. Under such circumstances it was not long before 55013 *The Black Watch* was withdrawn on 20 December, after sustaining an engine failure in the London area. Withdrawal was pronounced at Finsbury Park Depot and it was here that it languished until a tow to Doncaster Works was available.

From now on it was 'every "Deltic" for itself', for its next major failure would mean imminent withdrawal. Sure enough, such a failure befell 55010 *The King's Own Scottish Borderer*, which had been in trouble for a few weeks. These troubles multiplied, eventually culminating in its removal to Doncaster Depot after throwing oil from one power unit and having fractured a cylinder liner on the other. The locomotive's withdrawal took effect on Christmas Eve.

By now the 'Deltics' were deteriorating day by day to such an extent that, on 22 December, 55016 *Gordon Highlander* was stopped at Peterborough after sustaining fire damage. It was not long before 'Deltic' '16', the pride of the 'Deltic Devonian' rail tour, was returned to York Depot, where it was withdrawn due to the fire damage and several other defects on 30 December. Up until that time it was common knowledge that *Gordon Highlander* had been the 'Deltic' Preservation Society's first choice for preservation, due amongst other factors to its overall sound body condition, so this fire damage along with the other defects was certainly catastrophic. The Society's only course of action now was to start to assess the next best member of the class for preservation. Meanwhile, 55016 lay at York awaiting removal to Doncaster Works.

Its race now run, withdrawn 'Deltic' 55010 The King's Own Scottish Borderer *awaits cutting up at Doncaster Works* (S. Cholmondeley).

On 30 December, my own personal favourite 'Deltic', 55007 *Pinza*, ran into trouble whilst working the 08.05 York-King's Cross and had to be towed, along with its train, south from Newark to London by Class '47' 47146. The following day, 'Deltic' '7' was towed back to York from Finsbury Park Depot by Class '31' 31121. Upon arrival at York, *Pinza* was withdrawn and abandoned to await her last journey to Doncaster Works.

The same day was also to see the last working of a 'Deltic' over the cross-Pennine route to Manchester and Liverpool. The choice of power fell to the green-liveried 55002, which worked the 07.49 York to Liverpool. En route it was noticed that 55002 was throwing oil from one engine; it returned to York on the 12.05 from Liverpool and, after inspection, was withdrawn. *The King's Own Yorkshire Light Infantry* was lucky in being quickly removed to the National Railway Museum annex to face a new lease of life as an exhibit.

Thursday 31 December 1981 went down in railway history as the last day of regular service for the remaining 'Deltics' (55008/9/15/17/19/21 and 22). No 55022 *Royal Scots Grey* was sent north on the 05.50 King's Cross-Aberdeen as far as Edinburgh in preparation for its use on the final southbound 'Deltic Scotsman Farewell' special on 2 January 1982. No 55021 *Argyll and Sutherland Highlander* made its last run

Abandoned but not forgotten, my old friend Pinza *at the end of the road in Doncaster Works* (S. Cholmondeley).

on the 09.40 King's Cross to York and, although running on one engine only, made a creditable run north to York. Upon arrival, it made its last journey into York Depot. For 55008 *The Green Howards*, the last passenger journey was supposed to be the 14.03 King's Cross to York on the 31st, but in the event 'Deltic' '8' was failed with flat batteries by Finsbury Park Depot and Class '47' 47411 worked the train instead. That same night, 55009 *Alycidon* worked overnight to King's Cross to await the honour of being deputy and runner in front of the 'Deltic Scotsman Farewell' as far as Newcastle.

The honour of hauling the last regular northbound 'Deltic' service on 31 December befell 55017 *The Durham Light Infantry*. Besides the numerous enthusiasts present at King's Cross, there was also a Thames Television crew to record this momentous event. At 16.03, 55017 made her departure north heading for York. All the way north there were enthusiasts at the lineside to bid 'Deltic' '17' a fond farewell, and by the time Peterborough was reached, there were about 150 enthusiasts to greet the train. Meanwhile, 55015 *Tulyar* was thundering south on the last regular 'Deltic' southbound service into King's Cross, the 15.50 from York, but, due to a broken rail at Barkston, north of Grantham, the timetable was thrown into chaos. The decision was made to terminate 55017's northbound journey at Grantham and return the locomotive south. Unfortunately, 'Deltic' '17' expired at Knebworth on its way back and had to be helped on to London, eventually finding itself withdrawn at Finsbury Park Depot. After arrival at King's Cross, 55015 *Tulyar* was sent to Finsbury Park Depot to be prepared to haul the northbound 'Deltic Scotsman Farewell'.

Now there was only one 'Deltic' in regular service — 55019 *Royal Highland Fusilier*. This locomotive had a very busy last two days in service. It arrived south light engine on 30 December and then worked north to Aberdeen. On the 31st, 55019 was utilized on the 16.30 Aberdeen-York, where, on arrival at around 23.30, it made its lonely way to York Depot (and withdrawal), so bringing down the curtain on the regular use of 'Deltics' on the East Coast Main Line — the end of an era.

Now all was over, although there was to be one last curtain-call for the 'Deltics' — 'The Deltic Scotsman Farewell' special train on 2 January 1982. The honour of hauling this train was originally to have gone to 55002 *The King's Own Yorkshire Light Infantry'*, but to almost everyone's pleasure it fell upon 55015 *Tulyar*, which emerged from Gasworks Tunnel that morning into a packed King's Cross. Besides *Tulyar* gracing the actual train, 55009 *Alycidon* had been chosen to act as 'runner', travelling light engine from Peterborough some way in front of

The last 'Deltic'-hauled service train out of King's Cross prepares to leave behind 55017 The Durham Light Infantry, *31 December 1981* (D. Carter).

Tulyar as far as Newcastle in case of failure. To carry out this easy task, *Alycidon* was running on only one engine. The weather was atrocious for virtually the whole of the journey to Edinburgh (the train's destination) and rendered photography almost impossible, except for those owning the very best equipment. However, the weather did not deter the press and television companies from attending to record that momentous occasion, and *Tulyar* was undoubtedly the star of that damp Saturday morning. Throughout the day, *Tulyar* was screened to millions of television viewers all over the country on several news programmes.

The choice of motive power for the special was excellent — an ex-Finsbury Park 'Deltic' to work north and an ex-Edinburgh Haymarket locomotive (55022 *Royal Scots Grey*) to work the final southbound journey, each hauling 12 Mk I coaches. The choice of coaching stock was, I thought, wrong, however, Mk I coaches being restricted to a 90 mph maximum. Had Mk II coaches been made available sparks would really have flown when the two locomotives required that extra speed to recover from the several speed restrictions encountered on both runs. *Tulyar* itself, however, was in absolutely immaculate external condition, displaying white cab surrounds and with a nose end bedecked with a commemorative wreath, a very artistic cut-out 'Deltic'-shaped headboard and a more conventional one inscribed 'Deltic Scotsman Farewell'.

It was hard to believe that *Tulyar*'s final departure from Platform 7 was to be the last 'Deltic'-hauled train to leave King's Cross. A typical 'Deltic' performance ensued, with not a trace of wheel-slip up through the tunnels out of London on wet and greasy rails. Passing Potters Bar, *Tulyar* was doing 77 mph and once speed had reached the 90 mph mark, 'Deltic' '15' held on to it for the next 105 miles, almost to Newark. The highlight of the journey to this point was the topping of Stoke Bank at 87 mph with this approximately 455-ton train. Near Newark, *Tulyar*'s progress was temporarily halted, when a false signal triggered off a lineside hot axlebox detector. Once given the all clear, *Tulyar* passed Newark 5 mins late and, further on, a 30 mph permanent way restriction between Crow Park and Dukeries Junction caused the train to be 10 mins late at Retford. Onwards to the first crew-changing point at Doncaster, *Tulyar* exhibited more fine running up to 90 mph but was unable to regain all the arrears. It must have been very frustrating for the crew to know that here they had a locomotive quite capable of 100 mph plus, but were severely handicapped by the use of Mk I stock.

Tulyar departed from Doncaster 9 mins late, amidst an army of enthusiasts wishing her farewell, but she was soon hindered further by a lengthy 30 mph permanent way restriction at Arksey, after which commenced a lively run to York. Approaching York it seemed as though the whole of the city had turned out to see *Tulyar*. The station was crammed, and 55015 slid by exchanging pleasantries with well-wishers before opening up for the racing ground over the Great Plain of York. *Tulyar* took full advantage of this stretch, covering the 36 miles from Beningborough to Croft Spa in 24.1 mins, an average of just over 89 mph.

The next obstacle on the northbound journey was encountered on the approach to Darlington; *Tulyar* was slowed down and signalled through Bank Top Station itself, so being denied a fast passage via the station's outside high-speed through lines.

Away from Darlington, in the grips of freezing fog, *Tulyar* made an exemplary climb up to Bradbury Summit, at which point its vociferous engine noise could be heard for many a mile. Now only 5 mins late, speed continued on past Ferryhill, through Durham and across that magnificent viaduct giving such a panoramic view over the city towards the castle and cathedral, and on into the suburbs of Gateshead. At Gateshead's King Edward Bridge Junction, *Tulyar* swung its nose around the sharply curved turnout and squealed on to the King Edward Bridge, high above the River Tyne, for the last time whilst hauling a train. Once over the bridge, the train meandered into Newcastle Central Station for a final crew change.

This stop would be forever memorable, for on an adjacent track stood 55009 *Alycidon*, which had acted as a 'runner' all the way from London. *Alycidon* looked splendid, adorned with the ex-'Flying Scotsman' winged-thistle headboard, itself now a prized relic of the 1960s. Crews changed, *Tulyar* bid *Alycidon* farewell, and faced the continuation of the journey to Edinburgh knowing full well that no help was now at hand in front. *Alycidon* was by then being prepared to head off light engine south away from Newcastle for the last time in British Rail ownership.

The line from Newcastle to Edinburgh is not easy, abounding in restrictions of all types, but *Tulyar* made good use of its power and after a good run, culminating in 91 mph past Prestonpans, arrived in Edinburgh only 3 mins late. The moment *Tulyar* burst out of the tunnel at the

The final 'Deltic'-hauled train, the 'Deltic Scotsman Farewell', ran from King's Cross to Edinburgh behind 55015 Tulyar *on 2 January 1982. Throughout the journey the weather was atrocious but nowhere was it as bad as Bradbury, Co Durham, where* Tulyar *is seen emerging from freezing fog and snow, battling its way north in the fading light* (J. Flounders).

south of Edinburgh Waverley Station, the awaiting crowd erupted into rapturous cheers, which brightened up the cold, wet, miserable afternoon.

Meanwhile, all ready and waiting to haul the return train to London was 55022 *Royal Scots Grey*, looking an absolute treat and already bearing a headboard proclaiming 'Farewell to Thy Greatness'. No 55015 *Tulyar* then headed off towards Haymarket Depot, having first handed over the 'Deltic Scotsman Farewell' headboard and wreath to *Royal Scots Grey*, which was still embellished with its original number, D9000, along with its TOPS number 55022. The time at last came for 55022 to depart from Edinburgh, its first home, for the last time, and as *Royal Scots Grey* opened up no doubt many a tear was shed — in no time at all, 55022 had disappeared into the dark tunnel and was away south, leaving Edinburgh behind in a cloud of typical 'Deltic' fumes!

The Scottish border was soon passed, and *Royal Scots Grey* sped relentlessly on her final journey south, crossing the Royal Border Bridge at Berwick-upon-Tweed and speeding on through Northumbria. On the approach to Newcastle, darkness was setting in on a dreadful rainy evening. As *Royal Scots Grey* made its way towards Central Station for the last time, crowds of enthusiasts braved the inclement weather to bid a grand farewell to this proud old war-horse. Entering the station, 55022 faced a blinding array of flashlights from the hundreds of camera-clad enthusiasts who had taken over the platforms. For a time, police had a struggle to control the huge following, but things calmed down after *Royal Scots Grey* gave a mournful farewell on her horns and disappeared into the night.

Once clear of Tyneside, Co Durham flashed by and soon *Royal Scots Grey* was nearing Darlington. On the return journey, Bank Top showed no resistance and allowed 55022 down the high-speed through lines, avoiding the station. High speed ruled across the Plain of York, too, *Royal Scots Grey* proving to be master of the task in hand, and certainly not showing its age. Approaching York, the locomotive's latter-day home, speed eased off as 55022 calmly rounded the curve past the Motive Power Depot and came in sight of York Station. York, not to be outdone by Newcastle, was also alive with enthusiasts and as *Royal Scots Grey* passed beneath the cavernous roof, the whole station erupted!

Selby passed, Doncaster was next and proved no different, except for the sight of 55010 *The King's Own Scottish Borderer* standing forlornly awaiting entry into the works for scrap. Retford, Newark, Grantham and Stoke Summit all flashed by, and in no time at all 55022 was through Peterborough and across the River Nene.

Royal Scots Grey was scheduled to arrive at King's Cross at 20.02 and at 20.05, 55022 entered Gasworks Tunnel and emerged into King's Cross, horns blasting continuously as the train entered Platform 2. Mass hysteria broke out, both on and off the train. Cheering reached such a crescendo, echoing under the station roof, that it was almost deafening. One man, watched by millions on a television news programme, sank down on his knees and wept.

Stalwart of the southbound 'Deltic Scotsman Farewell', 55022 Royal Scots Grey *(note the York city crest above the number)* (D. Carter).

No 55022 *Royal Scots Grey* was now at rest at the buffer stops, well and truly the end of the line! To everyone's surprise, however, the driver of 55022 was far from finished — he shut down and started up her engines several times amidst much cheering! But she had to go. *Royal Scots Grey's* final lone departure from King's Cross must have been the saddest moment in the history of a locomotive class, a sight and sound which I think enthusiasts will never again witness. Slowly and with dignity, 55022 *Royal Scots Grey* slid out of the platform with hundreds of hands clinging to her side, not wanting her to leave — but in no time at all her mournful cries were lost in Gasworks Tunnel. The excitement now over, no time was wasted and 55022 headed north for York light engine to face imminent withdrawal.

No 55009 *Alycidon*, the 'Deltic Scotsman Farewell' stand-by, returned from Newcastle to Peterborough, and once 55022 had safely passed by heading south, *Alycidon* also made its way to York. No 55015 *Tulyar*, its work also now over, soon set off light engine from Edinburgh to Gateshead Depot. After a brief respite, the 'Deltic' bid Tyneside a fond farewell and slid off into the wet, dark evening, horns blaring, leaving behind many a tear in the eyes of the enthusiasts who had braved the chill northern air to catch a last sight of *Tulyar* leaving Gateshead.

Disposal and preservation

'The condemned 'Deltics' were shunted into a scrap line at the rear of Doncaster Works...'

British Rail now had only one thing left to do with the 'Deltics' — dispose of them — but first they had to be taken to Doncaster Works. It was a sorrowful sight to see these magnificent locomotives being towed one by one into the Doncaster area in funeral-like procession to await entry into the works.

In numerical order, the following describes the manner and time in which they departed York's Dringhouses Yard for Doncaster:

55004	left Dringhouses in tow at 10.15, 5 Jan 1982
55007	left Dringhouses in tow at 10.00, 4 Jan 1982
55009	left Dringhouses in tow with 55015, 55016 and 55022 at 09.05, 5 Jan 1982
55010	arrived at Doncaster Works at 14.20, 24 Dec 1981
55011	arrived at Doncaster Works at 16.05, 25 Nov 1981
55014	left Dringhouses in tow at 06.00, 4 Jan 1982
55015	(see 55009)
55016	(see 55009)
55018	arrived at Doncaster Works with 55011 at 16.05, 25 Nov 1981
55019	left Dringhouses with 55021 in tow at 09.18, 4 Jan 1982
55021	(see 55019)
55022	(see 55009)

It will be noticed that 55008, 55013 and 55017 are omitted from the above list. These three locomotives were withdrawn whilst on Finsbury Park Depot and eventually reached Doncaster on 22 January 1982, all three being towed together by 40020. 55010, being withdrawn direct from traffic, entered Doncaster Works bearing its one remaining nameplate, while all other 'Deltics' in the above list arrived without their nameplates.

Alas for *Ballymoss*, she was singled out to be the first of the batch to be cut up; work commenced on 12 January 1982. This 'Deltic' was for

Awaiting its fate, 55014 The Duke of Wellington's Regiment *stands next to Class '37' 37009 in Doncaster Works* (P. Crumpton).

many weeks during the latter end of 1981 the subject of many rumours regarding the possibility that John Cameron, the owner of Gresley 'A4' 'Pacific' *Union of South Africa*, was interested in preserving it, but this did not happen. Another rumour heard at York was that a South African businessman was also interested in buying *Ballymoss*, but in the end to the scrap-heap she went. The next 'Deltic' to be burned was 55014 *The Duke of Wellington's Regiment*, after which there was a short pause in the scrapping.

This was brought about because British Rail decided to allow Doncaster Works to hold an 'open day' for enthusiasts to pay a last homage to the surviving 'Deltics'. The date set for this 'last stand' was 27 February 1982. On view that day were 55002 (sent specially from the

National Railway Museum) 55004, 55005 (which was celebrating 12 months in the works having arrived on 21 February 1981), 55007, 55008, 55009 (displaying a self-adhesive *Alycidon* nameplate), 55010, 55011, 55013, 55015, 55016, 55017, 55019, 55021 and 55022. Although 55002 *The King's Own Yorkshire Light Infantry* had been towed to the works from York on Friday, 26 February, she was allowed to return to York under her own power later on the afternoon of the 27th. That day thousands turned out to view the 'Deltics'. Nos 55002, 55009 and 55019 were actually running and every few minutes opened up their engines, producing that vociferous roar and smoke effect. The general external cleanliness of most of the locomotives left a great deal to be desired, but visible effort had been made on 55015 *Tulyar* and the already preserved

Last stand for the 'Deltics' — Doncaster Works 'Deltic Farewell' Open Day, 27 February 1982. No 55008 The Green Howards *with 55010* The King's Own Scottish Borderer *make a sorry sight* (S. Cholmondeley).

55002. This very special day not only helped the organizers, but also the 'Deltic' Preservation Society (DPS) which, in a little over six hours, took £2,000 at their makeshift sales stand.

The DPS had the sole aim of buying, preserving and running a 'Deltic' in working order. It had been common knowledge for a long time that the Society had set itself up to purchase 55016 *Gordon Highlander*, but after that locomotive had sustained fire damage, along with other defects, it was no longer a viable proposition. The DPS now had the arduous task of choosing an alternative. After many hours of sustained effort, it was decided that 55019 *Royal Highland Fusilier* was the best buy. During February 1982, the DPS received a tender form from British Rail offering 13 'Deltics' for sale. DPS members receive a bi-monthly magazine entitled 'Deltic Deadline' and in the February 1982 edition appeared an urgent plea to send donations to buy a second 'Deltic' — this time a 'racehorse'. This gave me much personal joy, for I thought *Pinza* might be saved, but it was not to be. I must confess that the DPS took the correct decision when they chose 55009 *Alycidon*. On 4 March the completed tender form was handed to the Director of Supply,

Derby, requesting purchase of 55009 and 55019.

The condemned 'Deltics' were shunted into a scrap line at the rear of Doncaster Works, where they became subjects of much vandalism by so-called enthusiasts. Eventually, to avoid the risk of further damage, 55009, 55015 and 55019 were separated from this line for safe keeping in a more concealed area of the works.

On 11 May 1982, it was confirmed that the DPS had been successful in the purchase of 55009 and 55019 for the sum of £38,065.20. This high price seems incredible for two redundant locomotives, taking into account the price paid for previously preserved diesels. The trouble with buying a 'Deltic', compared with say a 'Western' Class '52', is that a Class 52 is virtually 100 per cent scrap value upon withdrawal from service, whereas a 'Deltic' is not. Several 'Deltic' components are interchangeable with Classes '37' and '50', the largest items being the bogies themselves, so when buying a 'Deltic' complete, one is not necessarily purchasing scrap items. British Rail charged a price in accordance, which was bound to be higher in comparison with a Class '52' or '42' diesel-hydraulic locomotive.

Once purchased, both locomotives lost their original 'Deltic' bogies for use on Classes '37' and '50' and received bogies previously fitted to Class '37's. These bogies, once fitted, immediately downgraded the 100 mph speed of 55009 and 55019 to a maximum of 90 mph (but still adequate for secondary routes or preserved lines).

Once cut-up, 'Deltic' parts were utilized on other classes (the largest items being the bogies). Here is 37009 at Darlington running on 'Deltic'-type cast bogies (S. Cholmondeley).

Upon completion of specialized work in Doncaster Works, 55009 and 55019 now awaited movement to their new home, the North York Moors Railway (NYMR). After much delay, the date for the movement of the pair from Doncaster to the NYMR was set for Friday 20 August, 1982, and on that date the hand-over ceremony took place in the con-

fines of the works' yard. Present at the occasion were dignitaries from both British Rail and the DPS. 55009 *Alycidon* had been reintroduced to her Finsbury Park white cab surrounds and 55019 *Royal Highland Fusilier* looked very clean, both locomotives bearing their respective replica nameplates. Prior to the ceremony, both had acquired a considerable amount of grime after many months of disuse, so their prime external condition for this occasion must have been the culmination of many hours' work in the Doncaster shops.

Once the official speech-making was over, it was the duty of the then DPS Chairman, David Carter, after many years of hard work for the Society, to 'flag away' 55019, followed by 55009, both bearing DPS headboards. Noticeable were the tones of the horns on both 'Deltics', for they had, through lack of spares, been fitted with Class '50' examples. Happily it was not long before both 'Deltics' were reunited with horns of the correct pattern. After reaching the works' boundaries both locomotives' engines were shut down; a brake van was attached to the rear of 55019 and Class '37' 37100 was coupled up ahead of 55009. All couplings having been checked, the convoy departed from Doncaster at 14.00. The route chosen was via Shaftsholme Junction, Knottingley, Church Fenton, York, Northallerton, Eaglescliffe and Bowesfield Junction, to reach Thornaby Depot, Cleveland.

No 55009 Alycidon *stands in Grosmont Depot, North Yorkshire Moors Railway, 18 May 1985* (H. Watson).

Everywhere along the route, enthusiasts had congregated to pay homage to the finest class of diesel locomotive to grace the East Coast Main Line. Fortunately, Thornaby Depot had the good sense to position the two 'Deltics' at the side of the access road leading from the depot's entrance on the busy Stockton-on-Tees to Middlesbrough road. This foresight saved any over-enthusiastic spectators risking life or limb to get a look at both locomotives. Obligingly, the staff of Thornaby also allowed the public on to the access road to take photographs — a gesture much appreciated.

The next part of the movement took place on Saturday 21 August. At the crack of dawn, another Class '37' (37005) made its way out of Cleveland towing both 'Deltics'. No 37005, itself older than both 'Deltics', had a double towing job that day — once it had delivered 55009 and 55019 safely to Grosmont, it returned to Thornaby towing a failed Class '31' that had expired while on loan to the NYMR.

Now on NYMR property, it was not long before 55019 sprang into life, followed later by *Alycidon*. At 10.55, *Royal Highland Fusilier* departed Grosmont on the first ever 'Deltic'-hauled train to traverse this undulating line to Pickering. On this first trip, 55019 was reduced to a 'snail's pace' at Green End Bridge and again at the road bridge in Goathland; this was to ascertain clearances for Class '55' operation. In fact, so close were the clearances that it is very doubtful that should 55019 be restored to original two-tone green livery her horns will be fitted to their original position on the cab roofs. This situation will not affect *Alycidon*, which was never fitted with roof-mounted horns. In the end, all went well and Class '55' operation went ahead.

Needless to say, the 'Deltics' were such consistent crowd-pullers that the NYMR's fare takings during the 1982 season went up by 10 per cent. This location has given the British-based members of the DPS the opportunity not only to see their locomotives, but also to visit the magnificent surrounding countryside through which this railway runs. Moreover, Grosmont is more or less halfway up Britain's East Coast, so London in the south is as close to the NYMR as Dundee in Scotland is from the north — an ideal location. It is also possibly the only preserved line in the country which can give the 'Deltics' the 'work out' they require — they are high-revving machines that love to be thrashed, and the ideal gradient profile of the NYMR, along with its numerous curves and well-laid straights, combine to make it the obvious home for these locomotives — and long may they enjoy it!

Meanwhile, back on the Doncaster Works' scrap line, events had not stood still. The next 'Deltic' to be cut up was 55010 *The King's Own Scottish Borderer* during May 1982. June came and went with no further scrappings and by mid-July 55004/5/7/8/11/13/15/16/17/21 and 22 were

The end very near — 55010 festooned with affectionate graffiti (S. Cholmondeley).

still intact. During June, Euston's 'Collector's Corner' boasted the sale of the cut-out cabside data panel and number 55018 of *Ballymoss* for £25, along with various other 'Deltic' bits and pieces.

In July, 55007 *Pinza* was cut up. *Pinza* had earlier been a possible candidate for preservation by a firm of printers in the Wetherby area; apparently the owner of the firm had an interest in racehorses and would have liked *Pinza* as a static display outside his premises, but due to permission being denied by the local authority the idea was dropped. The next two 'Deltics' to face the cutter's torch were 55008 *The Green Howards* and 55021 *Argyll and Sutherland Highlander*. The former's No 2 end cab was to survive in a most unusual fashion, being purchased, complete with buffers etc, and weighing 5 tons, by Paul Lambeth from Chipping Norton, Oxfordshire. His acquisition left Doncaster Works on Thursday 26 August aboard a low-loader lorry. Upon arrival at Chipping Norton, the cab was put in storage pending restoration to two-tone green livery.

Likewise, 55021 was cut up and Kevin Cox of Steeton, near Keighley, West Yorkshire, purchased the No 1 end cab for private exhibition in his garden. Mr Cox took delivery by road transport on Wednesday 15 September 1982, and television news featured the sad sight of 55021's cab, after being transferred from the low-loader to a tractor and trailer, being propelled across a meadow towards Mr Cox's garden. The survival position by September 1982 was 55004/5/11/13/16/17 and 22, 'Deltic' '15' *Tulyar* being kept aside for possible future preservation.

On 11-12 September 1982, Carlisle Upperby Depot staged a public open weekend. Special guests among the usual classes of locomotives were Class '40' 40122 (renumbered 200), the green-liveried 40106, Gresley 'A4' 'Pacific' 4498 *Sir Nigel Gresley* and the immaculate 55002 *The King's Own Yorkshire Light Infantry* from the National Railway Museum, York. No 55002 was hauled dead to Carlisle and apparently remained that way as a static exhibit all weekend. The return journey was by means of inclusion in a Carlisle to Tyne Yard freight, hauled by 37071, on 13 September. It was next noted in Tees Yard before being towed off to York.

By the late autumn of 1982, 55015 *Tulyar* had been standing around Doncaster Works so long and had begun to look more dejected each month due to the weather and parts removed, that enthusiasts began to express concern about its future. Eventually Christie's, the auctioneers, set a date of 16 December for *Tulyar* to be sold by public auction at their London salesroom. A reserve price of £10,000 was put on the locomotive, but on the day the bidding came to no more than a little over £5,000, so *Tulyar* was withdrawn from the sale to spend the remaining part of 1982 with a very large question-mark hanging over her future.

The next 'Deltic' to be cut up was 55011 *The Royal Northumberland Fusiliers*, which by mid-October had been de-fuelled and positioned ready for dismantling. However, it had a few weeks' reprieve when the

No 55011 shorn of all dignity at the end of its life (P. Crumpton).

cutter's torch was directed instead to some withdrawn coaching stock. No 55011 was eventually broken up during mid-November 1982.

December 1982 was a month of rejoicing at Doncaster Works with the official launching on 9 December of their first Class '58' freight locomotive. Meanwhile, as work progressed on the Class '58' project during that festive month, at the rear of the works the cutters had once more been busy. This time it was on 55013 *The Black Watch*, affectionately known by Driver Harry Wilson of York Depot as 'Blackie'. No 55013 was Harry's favourite 'Deltic' and his greatest accolade to her was written in a touching passage by him in a copy of 'Deltic Deadline'. A sad loss, indeed, and an excellent performer in her day.

So out went 1982 and in came 1983 with only 55004, 55005, 55016 and 55017 awaiting cutting up. *Tulyar* was still awaiting the next decision on her fate, when another 'Deltic' joined her on the 'for sale' line — 55022 *Royal Scots Grey*. By early January 1983, an established Bournemouth-based group had made their intentions clear to raise up to

£22,000 to secure *Royal Scots Grey* for eventual use on the Nene Valley Railway, Peterborough. 'Deltic 9000' Fund Secretary, Michael Timms, received official tender forms from British Rail in January 1983.

During that month the cutter's torch burned into 55017 *The Durham Light Infantry* and by the end of the month work had started on cutting up 55005 *The Prince of Wales's Own Regiment of Yorkshire*. Also back on the tender list was the never-say-die 55015 *Tulyar*. A group of interested persons, known as the 'Tulyar Locomotive Club', with Chairman Robert Griffiths of Stoke-on-Trent, set about the task of purchasing *Tulyar* by issuing £50 shares to save all or part of 'Deltic' '15'. Whatever transpired between British Rail and the Club is not clear, but *Tulyar* was to remain deteriorating outside Doncaster Works for many more months.

Meanwhile, Mr Timms of 'Deltic 9000 Limited' had successfully tendered for 55022 *Royal Scots Grey*, and during late April restoration work started, one of the first jobs apparently being the exchange of its bogies for those of 55004 *Queen's Own Highlander*. Finally, during the summer of 1983, a surprising incident took place at Doncaster Works when 55015 *Tulyar* and 55016 *Gordon Highlander* were both removed from the works' scrapping schedule. This only left poor old 55004 to be disposed of, scrapping taking place during July.

One of the happiest occasions at Doncaster Works during 1983 was the farewell ceremony for 55022, now renumbered 9000. On Wednesday, 7 September, *Royal Scots Grey* was positioned in front of the Crimpsall Shop on the nicknamed 'lawn' part of the works. Resplendent in a fresh coat of paint and with nameplates fitted, the locomotive gave a healthy roar before running up the yard. After all the previous speculation about the creditability of her mechanical condition, 9000 sounded perfect and was in full operational condition. For the occasion it was adorned with the 'Flying Scotsman' train 'winged thistle' headboard, loaned specially by the National Railway Museum. The next day, 8 September, saw the sad, yet happy, sight of Doncaster's last operational 'Deltic' leave for its new home on the Nene Valley Railway, Peterborough, towed by Class '31' 31102.

A little later, on 23 September, 1983, *Royal Scots Grey* represented the 'Deltics' at the Norwich Crown Point Open Day instead of 55002 *The King's Own Yorkshire Light Infantry*, being towed to Norwich and back from Peterborough.

Now only two 'Deltics' survived at Doncaster — 55015 *Tulyar*, still surviving under a preservation bid but looking even more forlorn, and 55016 *Gordon Highlander*, in a terrible state but now living in hope after a preservation bid had been received during September.

September 1983 also found 55002 *The King's Own Yorkshire Light Infantry* at Workington Depot Open Day on the 10th in the unusual company of D1041 *Western Prince*, 40122, 45043, 20189 and 26031. No 55002 was towed both to and from the venue. It was also a really nice gesture by British Rail to consider a now-preserved diesel for exhibition

'Deltic' 9000 Fund's Royal Scots Grey *happy in retirement at the 1985 'Scotrail' Exhibition* (H. Watson).

in Scotland, taking into consideration the cost and time involved in towing the locomotive (55002 again) from its York base to the Ayr Depot Open Day on 29-30 October. Along with the usual Scottish diesel and electric representatives, *The King's Own Yorkshire Light Infantry* stood among steam locomotives *Union of South Africa, Flying Scotsman* and *Duchess of Hamilton*. It had travelled up to Ayr on 26 October as part of the 18.21 Whitemoor to Mossend Speedlink from York to Tyne Yard, making its way further north two days later on the 04.21 Tyne Yard to Stranraer Speedlink, hauled by Class '40' 40034 *Accra*. No 55002 returned to York on 31 October behind the green-liveried 40122 on the 15.55 Stranraer to Scunthorpe freight from Falkland Junction, Ayr, to York.

much speculation when she was towed out of Doncaster Works and away to Derby Research Centre. The official reason for this move was that *Tulyar* was to undergo dynamic tests to its bogies. During these tests 55015, on paper anyway, acquired the number 977177. *Tulyar*'s stay at Derby was to be brief, and during early 1984 it was announced that a Peter Sansom of Leicestershire had purchased 'Deltic' '15', and *Tulyar*'s new home was to be the Midland Railway Trust, Butterley, near Derby. Subsequently, the 'Deltic' Preservation Society has purchased 55015 from Peter Sansom and also acquired the cab of 55008 *The Green Howards* to use as a mobile exhibition unit, fitted on to a low-loader-type road trailer. The cab has been fully restored by Derby Works apprentices to two-tone green livery, and has been numbered D9008.

With 55015 *Tulyar* now safely out of danger, the honour of being the last 'Deltic' at Doncaster Works fell upon *Gordon Highlander*.

'Deltic' gravestone? No, just the original nameplate of D9001 St Paddy *out to grass (H. Watson).*

Towards the end of 1983 it had become known that 'Deltic' '16' had, in fact, been successfully tendered for and was eventually to join 9000 *Royal Scots Grey* on the Nene Valley Railway.

The 'Deltic' era under British Rail ownership having now ended, one can only hope that 9000, 55002, 55009, 55015, 55016 and 55019 can survive the rigours of preservation and pass from generation to generation to keep that unmistakable 'Deltic' sound alive.

Appendix I

General details and specifications

Introduced 1961
Manufacturer English Electric, Vulcan Foundry, Newton-le-Willows, Lancs
Route availability 5
Maximum service speed 100 mph
Wheel arrangement Co-Co
Weight 100 tons (in running order)
Power classification Type 5
Tractive effort 50,000 lbs
Length 69ft 6in
Width 8ft 9½in
Height 12ft 10in
Wheelbase 58ft 6in
Driving wheel diameter 3ft 7in
Engines 2 Napier 'Deltic' series D18-25 of 1,650 bhp at 1,500 rpm
Brake horsepower 3,300
Cylinders Bore 5.125in, stroke 7.25in x 2
Transmission 6 English Electric type EE538A axle-hung nose-suspended electric traction motors
Main generator English Electric type EE829-1A
Auxiliary generator English Electric type EE913-1A
Fuel tank capacity 900 gallons
Lubricating oil capacity 50 gallons
Cooling water capacity 33 gallons
Boiler water capacity 640 gallons
Boiler type 'Spanner' Mk II
Type of brake air/vacuum
Brake force 51 tons

Appendix II

Numbers, names and naming locations

The naming of the 'Deltics' allocated to Finsbury Park Depot, London, admirably carried on the old LNER tradition of naming some of its prestigious locomotives after racehorses. The Gateshead-based 'Deltics' were given the names of local North-East regiments, some of which had previously adorned LNER 'V2' and LMS 'Royal Scot' steam locomotives. Likewise, Edinburgh Haymarket Depot also opted for regimental names, featuring Scottish regiments.

Original number series D9000-D9021
Interim number series (after abolition of steam locomotives) 9000-9021
Final TOPS numbering 55001-55022

Original No/ TOPS No	Name	Date of naming	Location of naming
D9000/55022	*Royal Scots Grey*	18/6/62	Edinburgh Waverley
D9001/55001	*St Paddy*	7/7/61	Doncaster
D9002/55002	*The King's Own Yorkshire Light Infantry*	4/4/63	York
D9003/55003	*Meld*	7/7/61	Doncaster
D9004/55004	*Queen's Own Highlander*	23/5/64	Inverness
D9005/55005	*The Prince of Wales's Own Regiment of Yorkshire*	8/10/63	York
D9006/55006	*The Fife and Forfar Yeomanry*	5/12/64	Cupar
D9007/55007	*Pinza*	22/6/61	Doncaster
D9008/55008	*The Green Howards*	30/9/63	Darlington Bank Top
D9009/55009	*Alycidon*	21/7/61	Doncaster
D9010/55010	*The King's Own Scottish Borderer*	8/5/65	Dumfries

Original No/ TOPS No	Name	Date of naming	Location of naming
D9011/55011	*The Royal Northumberland Fusiliers*	28/5/63	Newcastle Central
D9012/55012	*Crepello*	4/9/61	Doncaster
D9013/55013	*The Black Watch*	16/1/63	Dundee
D9014/55014	*The Duke of Wellington's Regiment*	20/10/63	Doncaster
D9015/55015	*Tulyar*	13/10/61	Doncaster
D9016/55016	*Gordon Highlander*	28/7/64	Aberdeen
D9017/55017	*The Durham Light Infantry*	29/10/63	Durham
D9018/55018	*Ballymoss*	24/11/61	Doncaster
D9019/55019	*Royal Highland Fusilier*	11/9/65	Glasgow Central
D9020/55020	*Nimbus*	12/2/62	Doncaster
D9021/55021	*Argyll and Sutherland Highlander*	29/11/63	Stirling

Appendix III

Delivery and withdrawal dates

Number	Delivery date	Withdrawal date
D9000	28/2/61	2/1/82
D9001	23/2/61	5/1/80
D9002	9/3/61	30/12/81
D9003	27/3/61	31/12/80
D9004	18/5/61	28/10/81
D9005	25/5/61	8/2/81
D9006	29/6/61	8/2/81
D9007	22/6/61	31/12/81
D9008	7/7/61	31/12/81
D9009	21/7/61	2/1/82
D9010	24/7/61	24/12/81
D9011	24/8/61	8/11/81
D9012	4/9/61	19/5/81
D9013	14/9/61	20/12/81
D9014	29/9/61	22/11/81
D9015	13/10/61	2/1/82
D9016	27/10/61	30/12/81
D9017	5/11/61	31/12/81
D9018	24/11/61	13/10/81
D9019	29/12/61	31/12/81
D9020	12/2/62	5/1/80
D9021	2/5/62	31/12/81

Appendix IV

Allocations

	To Finsbury Park	To Haymarket	To Gateshead	To York
D9000	-	2/61	-	5/79
D9001	2/61	12/67-6/68*	-	-
D9002	-	-	3/61	5/79
D9003	3/61	12/67-6/68*	-	-
D9004	-	5/61	-	5/79
D9005	-	-	5/61	5/79
D9006	-	6/61	-	5/79
D9007	6/61	-	-	6/81
D9008	-	-	7/61	5/79
D9009	7/61	12/67-6/68*	-	5/79
D9010	-	7/61	-	5/79
D9011	-	-	8/61	5/79
D9012	9/61	12/67-6/68*	-	6/81
D9013	2/68-6/68*	9/61	-	5/79
D9014	-	-	9/61	5/79
D9015	10/61	-	-	6/81
D9016	12/67-6/68*	10/61	-	5/79
D9017	-	-	11/61	5/79
D9018	11/61	-	-	6/81
D9019	12/67-6/68*	12/61	-	5/79
D9020	2/62	-	-	-
D9021	11/64-6/65*	5/62	-	5/79

* Temporary allocation

Index